Looking for Love at 82

ALEX GALL

Copyright © 2020 by Alex Gall.

ISBN   978-1-970160-86-4 Ebook
ISBN   978-1-970160-87-1 Paperback

All rights reserved. No part of this publication may be reproduced, distributed, or transmitted in any form or by any means, including photocopying, recording, or other electronic or mechanical methods without the prior written permission of the publisher. For permission requests, solicit the publisher via the address below through mail or email with the subject line "Attention: Publication Permission".

The EC Publishing LLC books may be ordered
through booksellers or by contacting:

EC Publishing LLC
116 South Magnolia Ave.
Suite 3, Unit F
Ocala, FL 34471, USA
Direct Line: +1 (352) 644-6538
Fax: +1 (800) 483-1813
http://www.ecpublishingllc.com/

Ordering Information:
Quantity sales. Special discounts are available on quantity purchases by corporations, associations, and others. For details, contact the publisher at the address above.

Printed in the United States of America

Dedication

To my late wife Anna,
she was the best thing that ever happened to me.

Contents

Dedication iii
Introduction xiii
Preface xv

Looking For Love at 82 1
Profile – Describing Yourself 3
The Basic Dating Plan is Free 6
Love: What is it All About? 8
The Women On the Computer Dating Service - A Different Perspective 9
Education Level of Women on Computer Dating 18
Love and Aging 19
Repeated Reasons, Motivators and Goals in the Profiles of Women . 20
Women on Computer Dating 21
Profiles in General 22
The Use Of Attention In An "About You" Section of a Computer Dating Profile 27
What Price Success? 28
Smoking, Alcohol Drinking, Exercise and Diet 29
Telephone Dating (Somewhat Redundant About Me) 30
A Few Memorable "About Me" Remarks 31
Random Comments in the "About Me" Section of Profiles 32
My Dating Profile 33
Profiles and "About Me" Revisited 35
Discussing the "About Me" Section of Women's Profiles 35
Sweat the Small Stuff 38
Love Your Spouse 42
Final Thoughts 43
To My Late Wife, Anna Gall a Tribute
Goodbye Anna, Anna Goodbye but not Forgotten 44
Is It Charitable Gambling? 55

PLUS (ESSAYS)

Epilepsy..57
Hooray for Radio..59
The Mosque 62
My Favorite Sandwich 66
Modern Elections...67
Clutter 68
Mystery Telephone Call..70
Mail Intimidations 70
Accountants 73

JOKES

Acting...73
Adam and Eve...73
Airplanes...73
Alcohol..73
Ambition...74
Anger 74
Animals...75
Anxiety 77
Appearance 77
Arguing...77
Arithmetic...78
Art 78
Automobiles..78
Banking...79
Barbers..80
Baseball...80
Beauty...80
Boxing 81
Brains..81
Business 82

Candy	82
Cannibals	82
Cards	83
Charity	83
Christmas	84
Cleaning	84
Clothes	84
Coal	84
Coffee	85
Compliment	85
Condiments	85
Cooking	85
Cowboys	85
Crime	86
Cursing	86
Dancing	86
Dating	87
Death	88
Debating	89
Deliveries	89
Dentists	89
Doctors	89
Dracula	90
Dreams	90
Economics	90
Education	90
Efficiency	92
Eggs	92
Electricity	92
English	92
Entertainment	92
Environment	93
Evolution	93
Exercise	93
Fairy Tales	93

Family	93
Farming	94
Fashion	94
Fishing	95
Flowers	95
Food	95
Frankenstein	97
Friends	97
Furniture	98
Gambling	99
Games	99
Gardening	99
Ghost	100
Gold	100
Golf	100
Hair	100
Halloween	100
Handwriting	100
Happiness	101
Health	101
Height	102
History	102
Humor	103
Identity	103
Insults	103
Insurance	103
Inventions	104
Justice	104
Laundry	104
Lawyers	104
Laziness	104
Lies	105
Life	105
Light Bulbs	105
Living	105

Love	105
Luck	107
Magic	108
Mail	108
Management	108
Manners	108
Marriage	109
Mathematics	110
Medicine	110
Mercy	110
Military	111
Modesty	111
Money	111
Mood	113
Mummies	113
Music	113
Names	113
News	114
Nudists	114
Observations	114
Painting	115
People	115
Personality	115
Physicians	115
Plants	116
Plumbers	116
Police	116
Politics	117
Pool	118
Problems	118
Psychics	118
Psychologists	119
Reading	119
Religion	119
Revenge	120

Role Models	120
Rumors	120
Running	121
Safety	121
Sales	121
Seafood	121
Seniors	122
Shoes	122
Shooting	122
Shopping	122
Signature	122
Silence	123
Singing	123
Sleep	123
Smoking	124
Space	124
Speaking	124
Speech	124
Spiders	125
Sports	125
Statues	127
Strength	127
Success	127
Telephone	127
Television	127
Thinking	128
Time	128
Trash	128
Travel	129
Vanity	129
Vision	130
Waiters	130
Wall Street	130
Weather	130
Weight	131

Work	131
Wrestling	134
Writing	134
Zombies	135

Introduction

My wife of 57 years passed away in July 2019 the victim of the Alzheimer malady. I was devasted. I loved my wife. We had no children. We never argued and I felt comfortable in her presence; she was a wonderful woman. Anna was a Seventh Day Adventist (SDA). We married as Catholics, but she became interested in the SDA religion and decided to change religions. At first, I questioned the change but since I could see that the change made her happy, a condition that I liked I demurred. My goal as a husband was to see to it that my wife was happy. Happy wife, happy life. It was not too difficult adjusting to her change of religions; in fact, I liked it. SDA people follow tenets of the Old Testament, but don't quote me. They observe the Sabbath on Saturday, do not wear jewelry and do not eat unclean foods primarily pork and fish without scales. SDA members try not to drink alcohol or smoke and they tend to live a long time. With their no jewelry dictum, my wife promptly removed her wedding ring. Rather than grouse and pout I removed my wedding ring. My paramount goal was the happiness of my wife. I survived the wedding ring removal, since I looked single without the wedding ring. I thought I would be inundated with attention from single women or frustrated love-starved separated, estranged, divorced or widowed women but to my amazement none of this occurred. I managed to survive this phenomenon despite the fact that I may have lost my magnetic charm which I am looking for high and low, mostly low. I could not believe that I wasn't a chick magnet, a legend, in my own mind.

When my wife passed away, I wrote a tribute to her. I was no pharaoh. I could not build a pyramid or an obelisk or a huge tomb or whatever the local pharaoh did to perpetuate his magnificence. In my case to honor my wife's memory I wrote the tribute so that people 10 or 1,000 years from now would be aware of my wife's existence, the beauty of her soul and that her husband loved her. That was my intention and as a thank you to Anna who was the best thing that ever happened to me. Anna made me a better person and will live in my memory until

I pass away and be forgotten along with the countless of others who preceded me.

I had my wife's tribute distributed for free on the social media network (whatever that is exactly being computer challenged). My step-brother Frank visits me periodically. I explained to him the premise of my new book entitled *Looking for Love at 82*. Frank listened patiently and when I was done, he suggested that I include my wife's tribute as the first chapter of the book since it was the reason for the book. Her passing had triggered my search for love at 82. Had Anna lived we would have still been happily married to each other. My step-brother was right; I had contemplated that and distribution on the social network and in the book while redundant furthered my goals.

On reflection I did not want to start the book on a somber note. I wanted to allow the lonely readers to look for love quickly by telling them how to proceed. My wife's tribute would follow and to brighten things up I would include and conclude with a section of original squeaky-clean jokes that were intended to leave readers in a good mood. The plan allows the book contents to proceed logically at least in my mind.

Well there you have it the evolution of *Looking for Love at 82*. The book in all its glory, my latest attempt at a legacy. A most humble attempt on my part to leave this world in a better state than when I found it. My attempt to bring happiness to individuals yearning and longing for love and to find happiness to brighten their futures and to give meaning and newfound hope and purpose in a world where solitude and loneliness abounds, and companionship and love promises an opportunity for happiness and a better life.

Preface

I was not anxious to write a preface, but I may be duty bound by custom. Can it be a desirable book without a preface? I don't recall a preface in the Bible, both the Old and the New Testaments, and they managed to survive through the ages without a formal preface.

It may be wise at this juncture to hurry because some people may be champing at the bit to press on to the text. I have known people who didn't bother to read any introduction or preface to a book that came to hand. I read all introductions and prefaces without fail. If I dislike either I have often skipped reading the book. I like to get the sense of how an author thinks. If that person's introduction is boring, too simplistic, too complicated or if they make little or no sense, why continue? An excellent introduction or preface will draw me in similar to iron fillings to a magnet, to continue. I find that the introduction is the key element for me. I admire any author who can make the introduction interesting and engrossing which is a reflection of the author's creative thinking process to follow.

Book reviews are often very useful. Strangely, I frequently forego reading the review of a book since I want to use my own judgement rather than relying on the judgement of others. I have occasionally abandoned reading a book if I have had to struggle through the first confused chapter.

There you have it, an unorthodox preface and technically not a preface at all. A preface has a plan or a goal outlining the gist of what is to come. Summarizing, the book is delightful since it is unique, humorous, funny at times, enlightening on occasion, clean and hopefully different. No one helped with the writing of the book. I am too unknown to merit a ghost writer. I may not have any skeletons in my closets either; how drab? Relax and enjoy the book. For people in the great country of Great Britain, cheers! Britain is great by definition, 'Great' Britain. Preface completed.

Looking For Love at 82

My wife of 57 years passed away in an assisted living facility in Aberdeen, Maryland on 25 July 2019. She was the victim of the Alzheimer malady. We had no children and the loss left me devastated. Happy wife, happy life. There was no one in my living area except my Maine coon cat, 'Cutie Pie'. The TV kept me informed but it was inanimate. The telephone merely reminded me that my car's warranty had expired and that I needed a security system and more life insurance. My late wife's Seven Day Adventist (SDA) church members stopped coming by and my few friends that I had worked with had moved away or passed away. I had outlived many of them. My living area was very quiet. The silence wasn't deafening because I couldn't hear it. The occasional telephone call literally woke up the dead. Its ringing was quite alarming. In a word after 57 years of happily married life I began to feel the pangs of loneliness. If it wasn't for my cat, Cutie Pie, I might as well have been a monk with a vow of silence.

I mentioned my sad state to my neighbor Ted. Ted, a Doctor of Law, was close to my age and one of my few friends. Ted was a tenant of mine. We lived in the same house in separate apartments for over five years. Ted was more than a tenant; he was a true friend in that we were both concerned with each other's welfare. Ted had been a bachelor for as long as I had known him. Knowing my plight Ted felt sorry for me and one day he stopped by to commiserate with me and offered up a suggestion. Ted said, "You know Alex, I signed up for a computer dating service. I submitted my profile describing my background, particulars and desires about the lady that I wanted to meet and in no time, I had dozens of inquiries. I did not follow up on the inquiries but Alex you would be surprised at the responses that I received. I had included a photograph of myself that I cropped from a family photograph. Why don't you try this computer dating service; you may be gratified at its effectiveness?"

I told Ted that I had put the word out through one of my late wife's Seventh Day Adventist's friends and elsewhere that I was looking for companionship either in person or on the telephone. I preferred a widow who was religious and did not smoke, do drugs other than prescription and was no more than a social drinker. I waited and waited but I did not hear a peep from my late wife's friends or anyone else for that matter. I said to Ted, "Ted, I'm at my wit's end." While I'm computer challenged, I did not even own a computer and I typed poorly. "How can I participate in computer dating?" Ted said, "Alex, you can use your tablet that I'll upgrade for you. You can prepare your profile and I'll take your photograph and include it with your profile." The plan was set in motion, but my success rate did not compare to Ted's results. Did I mention that Ted was a black minority? There are many attractive black women on the computer dating site. Ted was well educated. Perhaps Ted was head and shoulders above most of his competitors. As far as I know Ted never dated anyone who showed interest in him, but I may be wrong in that regard. Although I owned a crowbar I didn't like to pry.

I think that I received about six inquiries. In all of the people that I contacted and provided my telephone number to only one woman contacted me, and I received no dates. I rationalized my poor performance on two factors. First, I'm 82 years old. One woman stated that she was looking for a younger man and who can blame her? Second, I told the ladies that I had been using a walker since my stroke in 2015 and my mobility was reduced. Who can fault the ladies? Nearly all of them wanted to dance or go for long walks in the woods and that eliminated me. I wanted to walk and dance but could not keep up with a potential date. The ladies were right; I would have come to the same decision.

I revised my profile to include the walker information because I had to provide this information every time that I tried to get a date. Had I been younger and not on a walker I believe I would have been more successful. As it was, I came up empty – struck out. In the computer dating site one lovely lady replied that we were not a good match. Being rejected really hurt my ego and pride since I had never been rejected before. In my limited experience, I had dated about six women before I was married. I was no Casanova by choice. I wanted to be a one-woman

man to avoid comparisons and I was happy with my decision since it suited my nature. However, being rejected really hurt my ego. I told Ted of my plight and depression and Ted, being more worldly, cheered me up by telling me not to take it too seriously. By the nature of computer romance I had to expect rejection and I needed not to dwell on my failures. It was to be expected by the very nature of the experience. I needed to pick myself up, dust myself off and keep trying until success was attained. Just another life lesson for me proving that I had led a sheltered existence and being happily married for 57 years may had dulled my senses. That excuse satisfied my brain until I could come up with other rationalized excuses that were more original and creative similar to Groucho Marx, "If you don't like that excuse, I have others."

I must admit that reading the profiles of the lovely women available was quite habit forming. I found it very difficult to find a woman suited to my limitations. Most of the ladies wanted to dance, take long walks in the city, the woods or on the beach. I could just visualize myself with my walker legs slowly disappearing into the soft sand making walking difficult if not impossible. Other ladies wanted to go kayaking, biking, skiing and all manner of activities not conducive to a walker. What frustrated me was that I had taken Arthur Murray dance lessons during college and I could not put them to good use. Although I was no Fred Astaire, I could dance well enough not to embarrass myself. In addition, while working I jogged nearly every day during lunch for decades but on a walker, jogging was out of the question. In the hospital when I took the lung strength capacity test the floating air ball always reached the upper level on the device.

Reading the individual woman's profiles was entertaining, addictive and informative. Each profile had many categories to help to define an individual.

Profile – Describing Yourself

Every individual who wants to participate in the dating program has to describe himself or herself to allow potential dating partners to decide based on the information provided if there is any interest or attraction to the characteristics.

For review: a brief summary of the individual's characteristics is provided for informative purposes.

- Age
- Location
- Intent
- Profession
- Height
- Education
- Any children?
- For (term)
- Body type
- Religion
- Smoker?
- Ethnicity
- I am seeking
- Want children?
- Marital status
- Do you drink?
- Do you drive?
- Extended profile
- Do you have a car?
- Astrological Sign
- Hair Color
- Eye Color
- Pets
- Do you do drugs?
- Second language
- Gender
- Chemistry test (standard questionnaire)
- Longest relationship
- How ambitious are you?
- First name
- Interests (details)
- About me (often very detailed and informative)

Simple responses often posed problems. For example, marital status responses were:

➢ Single
➢ Separated
➢ Divorced
➢ Widowed

If a person is 75 and single what happened? Were they never married, divorced and now single or widowed and considered single? For the divorced, how many divorces? One divorce could be attributed to gambling, philandering, physical abuse, alcoholism, etc. If a person is separated is he or she still married or headed for a divorce? Has the couple been separated for one month or 10 years? How many children are involved, one or one dozen? If a person is a widow or widower when did it occur, one month or 10 years ago? A recent widow may not be over her grief and not ready for a serious relationship. In many instances widowed and divorced people have one or more, mostly more, children involved which reminds me of an old joke. John and Marsha were dating for one year. Marsha said, "John, I'd like you to have my children." John replied, "Marsha, how many children do you have?" With children there may be children, grandchildren and even great grandchildren. Children and grandchildren are the first love and responsibility of a parent and grandparents and rightfully so. Where does this leave the potential suitor? Some potential dates are grandmothers or even great grandmothers. A great grandmother may be under 80 years old. Being 82 years old an 80-year-old great grandmother is my age and can be attractive to me at 82 or have I alienated younger readers on this point? Am I supposed to date a 20-year-old and be branded a pervert or demented?

The most interesting attribute in the profile of potential daters involves personality. Responses to the category of personality are all over the map. A list of actual responses under the topic of personality is provided.

- Beach bum
- Animal lover
- I work
- Traveler
- Princess
- Hopeless romantic
- Physical
- Crafty
- Diva
- Rock star
- Adventurer
- Coffee snob
- Health care
- Film and TV junkie
- Tree hugger

Perhaps as interesting as personality is profession, a topic that had me laughing often. Fasten your seat belts.

- Union Carpenter
- Retail
- Business Development
- Banking
- IT Analysis
- Have one
- Programmer
- Nurse
- Medical
- It's really good
- Work
- Project Manager
- Cosmetology
- Romantic Assistant
- Dental Hygienist
- Music Snob
- Domestic Engineer
- Desk Jockey
- Geek
- Technical
- Plant Administrator
- Food Scientist
- Hospitality Industry
- Criminal Justice
- Recruiter
- A sticky one
- Ask
- I have a job
- I work hard
- Work for myself
- Appliance Specialist
- Traveler
- Business
- Self-employed
- Retired Fed
- Small cleaning business
- Legal
- Administrative Assistant
- Caregiver

The Basic Dating Plan is Free

For a price I could sign up for a larger selection of women; this is called an upgrade. There are several plans where the price increases as the size of the plan increases. In some instances, I was attracted to a lady who could only be contacted on an upgraded plan. The woman was on a plan that was more expensive. Was this tactic an attempt to shield these women who may have thought the members were poorer than upgraded plan payers? Are standard plan members considered riffraff? I was often greeted with a screen that said "Sorry" and my search ended then and there. As a standard member was I riffraff? What if I was worth millions? There may be some logic to their decision in an attempt to improve their lot in life. I could not contact the two women that I fell in love with based on their photograph and profile. How sad, requited love.

Under the topic of "Profiles" for me the most enlightening attribute is entitled "About Me." In "About Me" the potential date can expound at length regarding just about anything including what the candidate desired in a man, their special personality traits, a lady's personal philosophy of life, special requirements regarding their needs related to etiquette and treatment and all manner of pertinent topics. Deemed to be important topics include:

1. Intelligence of candidate
2. Degree of maintenance expected or required.
3. Male characteristics desired including skills, manners, wealth, health, physical attributes, philosophy, compatibility, attractiveness and friendliness, among others.

Not being able to contact my top selections really disturbed me and it still troubles me. I read only women's profiles. Women read male profiles. I am certain that a lot more information on computer dating exists and the search for companionship and love could be expanded easily and maybe I'll do that next if readers clamor for it or maybe someone will beat me to the punch. Either way it will be a surprise, then again if I remarry after finding love I'll be another statistic within the annals of human relations.

Specific comments in profiles are worth noting since they are often memorable, more to follow. The comments are not quoted verbatim but revised slightly for no specific reason.

1. If you voted for President Trump do not contact me, keep moving on.
2. If you live in a foreign country don't bother with me.
3. If you are a liar, a cheat or a scammer forget about me.
4. If you don't have transportation or want money, forget it. You won't get any money from me.
5. If you have a beard (ugh). A trimmed mustache is ok.

6. Include current photographs, no photo, no reply.
7. Use proper spelling and language.
8. Be sure to have all of your teeth in your mouth.
9. Do not include indecent photos or photos of you partially clad.
10. I am a progressive. (I loved this one.)

I could not upgrade my plan because I did not know my password and original email, while I can't blame the site owner, I felt cheated. They stole my future romance opportunity.

Love: What is it All About?

We have traveled a short way in our journey and quest. Love is a long road often littered with people who have been scammed, lied to, deceived, hood winked, victimized, fooled, mesmerized, hypnotized, cheated, swindled and duped. At this point I could use a thesaurus. Who is an expert concerning love? I have opinions on love, but your opinion may be better than mine because yours really counts; it is your future.

In my extensive review and reading of the computer profiles of women, I was a glutton to learn all that I could about what motivated a woman in her search for true love. I will list common themes, goals and desires that predominated what women were hoping to find, achieve and attain in their search for true love. I'll list some of loves attributes in no particular order since what is important to one person may not be critical or as important to another woman. Some of loves desirable attributes may be the same or similar for men but I read only women's profiles and no men's profiles. A women's opinion of men's desires for love may be better and more germane than mine since misjudging motivations, intentions, desires and goals may have dire consequences if a woman looking for love selects a loser rather than a winner. I was very lucky I was happily married for 57 years. It would have been longer, but I got outvoted by Alzheimers. I was asked on occasion, "To what do you attribute your happy marriage for 57 years?" I had a quick answer "I was very lucky I picked the right woman and that made all of the difference." As I said in the dedication to several of my books, "Marrying Anna, my late wife, was the smartest thing I ever did. I wish that I could do it again."

The Women On the Computer Dating Service - A Different Perspective

Good news gentlemen you are in for a pleasant surprise. I have read many profiles where the dating hopeful participants describe themselves in an attempt to attract, befriend, entice, schmooze, and charm to locate a man for a companion, a dating partner and sometimes a husband. As a recent widower I was beginning to get lonely and cast about to move on with my life after a happy 57-year marriage to my late wife Anna. I loved Anna. She was the best thing that ever happened to me. She was my life, the purpose of my existence. During our marriage my goal was to make her happy. I never cheated on her, never dwelled on the idea because I admired and respected her, and I did not want to break her heart. How could a man be married and cheat on a woman who does not cheat on him? I once read where a man shot his wife who had cheated on him rather than shooting her lover because she had broken her marriage vows and may do it again.

On my tablet I read, only today, where an unbelievable woman in the Midwest was actively creative by saying this paraphrased statement – My husband travels frequently and I'm not getting enough attention. I need attention and a lot more of it when he's gone for a lengthy period. As someone once said, "If I'm lying, I'm dying." When I read her plaintive plea, I was still grieving the loss of my wife. I had no intention of running the risk of being shot by a jealous, inattentive husband who was too busy with his job instead of stopping to smell and enjoy the roses. I was not quite desperately lonely, but I was lonely. Perhaps if I was never married, I would have hopped on a jet plane winging my way to the Midwest with lust in my being. Out of respect for my wife and my youthful Catholic school education beaten into me by sadistically cruel storm trooper like nuns. Just joking my cooler head prevailed. My lust was genuine, and the lady was so beautiful that I could readily and clearly face my dilemma because by choice I had always been a one-woman guy and I had convinced myself that I had in retrospect at the age of 82 made the proper choice. All through my life I had occasionally, personally seen and heard of cheating, incest, all types of philandering, cuckolding trysts and a myriad of heterosexual liaisons and orgies and I was a spectator never a participant. Was Oscar Wilde wrong about temptation, perhaps on occasion?

I realize that I have digressed straying from the primary topic of the ladies on the computer dating service, but it was by design or plan to digress anytime it, in my view, improves the book. Rest assured, when I'm done with this opinion piece, I'll have fully addressed the topic at hand and most of the questions that had existed in your brain will have been answered to your almost complete satisfaction or I'll be a monkey's inquisitive uncle.

Moving right along circuitously, why do people want to fall in love? Anyway, you knew that that issue would come up. The fact of the matter is that there is no one definitive and correct answer. If you held your breath until you had one answer that was 100 percent correct for every conceivable occasion your face would turn blue from a lack of oxygen and not from envy.

As I said earlier, I have read enough computer profiles that I will discuss ad infinitum later in this piece candidly. I became enamored with the profiles while sometimes somewhat boring and redundant, there were times a profile was almost brilliant. Have I lied to you before? Before what? I will admit readily that over my lifetime I have not read enough although I was an avid reader. If I had my way, I would have read more but needed time to eat and sleep. I would have read a whole lot more if I could have done so. In books people are doing things that I couldn't imagine, afford or much less consider seriously when it happened to someone else. I really enjoyed reading profiles vicariously and incredulously stories knowing full well that what transpired was amazingly interesting, informative, lucid, and with intermittent flashes of unexpected brilliance well worth the wait for it to pop up and to reveal its incredible memorable beauty in my mind rivaling anything that I have read in the past. Either I have not read enough in 82 years or what I have read was not classical enough or what I have written about, the flashes of brilliance, had merit.

Women's profiles that were written in an honest attempt to inform, lure, entice, snare perhaps that's too harsh a word but no worse than inveigle a suspecting man. A woman wants him to be a friend, a companion and ultimately the love of her life, her partner, her knight in shinning armor and her soulmate. The suitor becomes a role model, a lover, a father figure who possesses several qualities to complement the hopeful woman in a lifetime partnership the often-perfect match.

On a walker what ladies looked for in a courtship recently I did not possess for a variety of reasons. I was too old at 82 never too young, too rich or too poor, not fit enough, not healthy enough, not talented enough (I question that one), not dumb or smart enough. My friend was not as dumb as he looked but someone said the verdict was still out, that's why they make chocolate and vanilla. Not everyone wants the same thing in the end.

Luckily women's profiles were written with a purpose and good intentions. Love is not only desirable it is essential. Money and music are said to make the world go around. By the way, what does make the world go around? Think of the literature, the unbelievable often beautiful, wonderful and even haunting memorable musical lyrics that have been associated with love. When it comes to music where to begin? If you lived to 100 years you would still be trying to understand and explain what it is all about. Explaining love would take an eternity and no one lives that long.

Women who seek love are providing a necessary function. Ask a woman not married how often does she think about marriage. With some valid exceptions, the answer would be "every day or all of the time."

I used word 'soulmate' the goal or intention of the women to fulfill their desires, needs, aspirations, that they want to strive for and attain are pure and meritorious. After all the women are concerned with maximizing their happiness during their lifetime as well as the happiness of their family and anyone in their sphere and travels until the final trip into the unknown, uncertain future to reap their just rewards or to get what's coming to them.

I cannot blame any woman or man pursuing love. Can anyone get enough of it? Cause of death: Loved to death. I heard that you can be killed by kindness depending on the kind of kindness. Love is the glue that binds a great deal of human existence. I have repeated this joke for years. I heard it from either Henny Youngman or Rodney Dangerfield. I want to attribute it to give credit where credit is due. Joke: "My wife and I were happy for 21 years and then we met." Love fuels the economy. I don't want to dwell on this point because while correct and essential it is somewhat tangential, an important aside to the topic of the women on the computer dating service. At this point the reader either has forgotten or thought that I would never get around to or back to the topic at hand women on the computer dating service. The women who should be the lovely and intelligent, sincere and often brutal surprisingly blunt and frequently refreshingly candid and eloquent. I know that I've missed some descriptive adjectives, but I'm not done. Not by a long shot. There is plenty of book left to go and I'm in no hurry ladies, I'm only 82. While I'm at it in my experience with contacting ladies that I was attracted to my pride and ego had been hurt on many occasions. Men if you use the computer dating service forever or at least until Monday, with love be prepared for severe depression, a deflated ego, an unremorseful attack on your pride that could be deflated quicker than a safety pin bursting your colorful balloons assuming that you had the time or the stupid desire to inflate more than one (hire someone).

The lady causing my depression had the gall, and I use that name with tongue in cheek, which is exactly where it belongs. The lady had the nerve to say that I was too old for her. She was looking for a younger man. If she had been present I would have said, "I'm not old enough if we got married and I kick the bucket I believe you'll get at least half of or everything that I and my former, wonderful wife Anna had worked for and amassed or should I put that in my pipe and smoke it? At this point I should mention that I had the distinct pleasure of meeting the

Surgeon General of the United States, not some other surgeon general of some third world country, if they could afford one or even needed one. As it turned out the Surgeon General was a regular Joe. Coincidently his first name was Joe and his middle name was either Bolivar or Mary. I don't remember. That's right it was Mary and he swore me to secrecy not to disclose it because it made his dog embarrassed to have an owner, master (politically incorrect) named Mary. Well anyway the U.S. Surgeon General Joe, actually Mary, gave me an expensive Cuban cigar and he told me, and I quote, "Smoke it in good health but don't tell anyone who gave you the cigar." I agreed to the terms quickly since I had remembered that 60 years ago an engineer at Westinghouse Corporation had given all the draftsmen working on motor control blueprints a Cuban cigar on the occasion of the birth of his first son. I have to report that in 1976 I quit smoking all together. No, I wasn't in the altogether, I quit altogether. Back to the Cuban cigar I distinctly remember that the Cuban cigar was the best thing that I ever smoked in my life. Strike me dead if I'm wrong. I'm not going to pursue this train of thought because I'm straying again from our topic besides it doesn't add to it. In other words, it's not germane which is right next to France as I recall from high school geography. I get lost easily that's why I let other people drive. My friend became lost so easily that he couldn't find his way out of a telephone booth. The 911 people had to free him; it was awful.

I haven't forgotten the purpose of this exercise that is a different perspective on the lovely ladies on the computer dating service. Don't rush me, we'll get there in good time or at least before Social Security goes bankrupt. I'm only 82, I don't look a day over 81 ½. I could live to the ripe old age of 84. I would have had 84 years to fully ripen. I must be fully ripe. At that point I may have a will and most of my money will go to dogs, cats, horses, donkeys, wolves, burros, elephants and various and sundry critters that my late wife and I loved. That reminds me – what do you call a person in charge of a zoo? A zoopervisor. And a giraffe walks into a police station and says, "I want to report that my brother has been missing for three days." The officer at the desk asked, "What does your brother look like?" Or if you cross an elephant and a rhinoceros what is it called? An elephino. Finally, what does a dentist give you for one dollar? Answer: buck teeth.

Back to the women; you thought I forgot, didn't you? Don't be impatient. My late wife's genius foot doctor said, "If you are not patient you will soon become one." I'm a Type 'A' person. I said to the doctor, "Tell me something that I didn't know." I didn't want to be smart but I was on time for the appointment and he kept my wife and me cooling our heels for an hour in his waiting room and wouldn't you know it he had the gall had the nerve to charge Medicare, Aetna and me 1,000 dollars total to put a pad in one of my wife's shoes. The secretary told me that he did all his own billing. Either he didn't want to pay for financial help, or he didn't trust anyone. I'll never forget that bill. It was too much trouble and not my nature to rat him out or squeal. I'm no whistleblower or some other less distinguished name. Convicts call whistleblowers stool pigeons and we all know what stool is. The convicts have it right. Today whistleblowers want to become victims saying, "My life is threatened." Is that similar to throwing a hand grenade into a room, walking away and then eating a great meal at an upscale restaurant with a bottle of champagne followed by an expensive Cuban cigar and saying, "The brother of the guy that was killed by the grenade blast wants to get his hands on me?" Shouting "If I ever get my hands on you, I don't know what I'll do." Then came the cry, "I'm a victim. I'm being threatened, I fear for my worthless life. I need police protection."

Sorry about the digression but I warned you that it would happen, didn't I? I did not claim to be an expert on profiles, but I am a keen observer, as I'll explain. From my perspective women are preoccupied with informing potential dates of the music that they like. Music preferences are all over from jazz, opera, country and western, rhythm and blues, popular songs, oldies, et al. From my viewpoint rap music was usually disliked most for whatever reason but once in awhile I like rap if the lyrics are understandable and make some sense. Evidently a variety of music calms women, put them in a good mood, makes them happy, relaxed and comfortable while reducing nervous tension and stress. Music facilitates love and in that regard it's beneficial. I have to add when people are singing, I get a lot of requests, but I sing anyway.

Does it get any better than this? If I told you I was honest I would be lying. Can I get an amen?

Now for a touchy subject concerning interracial dating. Some ladies who are black women were matter of fact about dating. One said, "I will date both black and white men." One black lady was the most eloquent. I'll paraphrase it: God created man in his image, and we are all God's children and tolerate and get along with each other.

White women were more adamant concerning black men. Paraphrasing one white woman said, 'I'm waiting for my chocolate man to come along.' Another white lady said, "Are you surprised I only date black men?" I was a widower, single, and she was gorgeous, and I was out of luck discriminated against solely based on my skin color.

At first, I didn't read the profiles of black women but many of them were very attractive, educated, articulate and more desirable as my loneliness increased so did my longing. Was I tempted? You bet I was. I had never dated or kissed a black woman. I was never much of a Casanova with either black or white women. I can distinctly remember the tale about President Thomas Jefferson and his slave Sally Hemmings. She bore their children. As I recall Thomas Jefferson was about to be rejected following verbal attacks and criticisms by the opposition. Even 200 years ago the public was tolerant and understanding of what may have been love. President Jefferson took Sally and their son to France. When Sally set foot on French soil Sally and her son were free. The French didn't recognize or condone slavery. Sally and her son voluntarily returned to Monticello where she was a slave once more. I believe Sally was legally related through marriage on his wife's side of the family where a Scotch sailboat captain fathered Sally with the mother of Jefferson's wife. I may be misinformed but I read an account concerning Sally Hemmings. I understand Sally was a free woman returned to Monticello of her own accord. I did not want to believe that President Jefferson fathered a child with his slave, almost as bad as a President's telephone call to the Ukraine and charging the call to unsuspecting taxpayers. It would not be a bad idea if President Trump called the head of every United Nation's member.

I did not want to believe that President Jefferson Sally Hemmings story, but it sadly is true, several accounts and books have documented it. In my own mind I respected President Jefferson who was one of the founding fathers of our great country but evidently, he fathered more than our country. I prefer to believe, but cannot prove, that Thomas Jefferson and Sally Hemmings were married common law. They were together for many years. She didn't try to escape, as far as I know. Jefferson freed her. Beyond that what do I know? I suspect there might have been an element of love there somewhere. As an aside, I penned an essay on the topic of slavery in one of previous five books. The discussion of slavery was my own opinion. I am no historian, but my opinion may have been even better than others or I may be out in left field by myself. Here I go again off on a tangent as I warned but I have more to say about the women on computer dating and my search for love at the age of 82. Stay tuned.

Many of the ladies wanted and liked swimming. I was a good swimmer. I did laps for one hour which leads or allows me to relate a scene from an old William Bendik movie. Was I the only one who heard it? The scene was unforgettable. They were barbequing around the edge of a lake when out of the blue over a loudspeaker there was this announcement, "Will the lady who lost her bathing suit come out of the water? We found it."

Evidently there are many diverse reasons to cause people to fall in love. People as a pair complement each other. Happiness and joy are magnified, and pain, suffering and despair are minimized as a committed pair. When you are suffering alone no one is there to say, "Oh, poor baby" or "Let me kiss that for you" or "Does it hurt, show me where?" Men and women have an overwhelming desire to be nice to help one another. In a happy marriage this assistance is present on a more permanent basis, hence the expression, "I've got your back." Physical gratification is a part of a happy marriage with the idea of procreation as a goal for most people. Unexpected affection fulfills a need. Being married it's called love. In our society not being married it's called lust. Love and lust are strange bedfellows. Am I sorry I said that? Time will tell. What do you know a talking clock? I could use one of those because sometimes people won't give me the time of day.

I really like some of the comments in the 'About Me' portion of each profile. I will relate quirky 'About Me' comments later in another essay. There is something that I must get off my chest and it's not my t-shirt. At first, I read only the profiles of white women; there were plenty of them and I preferred them. I had dated only white ladies before. I had never dated or kissed a black woman; they were never around. Had I grown up where my neighbors were black and white, I may have had a crush on a beautiful black teenager if she liked me. Writing about black and white girls or women makes me somewhat uncomfortable. I prefer to use the word woman or women without any distinction and in a perfect world it may come to that eventually but not now. As I started to see the same white women frequently, I started reading the profiles of black women and I was in for an eye-opening surprise. Not only were many of them pretty but many had advanced degrees and were gifted writers. I was curious to learn all that I could as well as to see if I could detect any glaring differences. When it came to love the ladies of both races were quite similar. In many instances ladies of both races extended their virtues and more specific demands such as, "I won't tolerate a cheater, a liar or a scammer." Some lady said, "If you are going to act like a child go down to Toys R Us and buy some toys. More than one woman said, "If you like or voted for President Trump pass me by. We have nothing in common." Many women do not like President Trump based on the fact that he is an alpha male and not a wimp. President Trump is outspoken. While I like it, many are uncomfortable with his oratory. Uncomfortable and uneasy with his counterpunching techniques. I can vividly remember President Bush's press conferences when the press asked questions in an unruly, vile and vicious manner where each reporter tried to outdo each other in nastiness, shouting and a total lack of control. It was as if the rabble and mob mentality reigned supreme. I would have thrown reporters who disrespected the office of the president out on their ears. The few women reporters seemed more civil. I'm from New Jersey; I like counterpunchers. If you can't take the heat get out of the kitchen. No one wants to stop free speech, but a modicum of civility and decorum must be maintained and conformance to rules and regulations the order of the day. Childlike, immature actions which tend to magnify exponentially must be avoided. Disorder under President Bush and not President Carter happened review the tapes. What was good for the goose is good for the gander. If you can't act properly within the rules do everyone a favor and take your ball and leave. Get a job at McDonald's and see how long you will be around brow beating the customers. Can I get an amen? Keep counterpunching right makes might.

Education Level of Women on Computer Dating

The education level of the women on the computer dating program is nothing short of breathtaking. Most of the women had a bachelor's degree or more. The level of education ranged from high school to doctorate and even post doctorate. It is possible to send a message directly to someone that has a doctorate. The subject of the doctorate may not be detailed but where else can anyone have direct access to a person as credentialed as a woman doctorate with a picture included? Not just a doctor but an attractive woman. Can it get any better? You cannot tell a book by its cover was never truer, beauty plus brains. I could not easily correlate the education level of a woman with her appearance. I remarked, "She doesn't look like any doctor that I ever met." And yet the woman had post doctorate credentials. I was wrong often connecting a pretty face with the level of intelligence. Now that I'm a widower it could come in handy to connect a pretty face with a wealthy woman. I'm no psychic, but that works both ways. Selecting a wealthy man from a photograph could be an invaluable talent for any woman who desires wealth. Imposters and scammers, male and female prey on good hearted, honest, gentle, desirable computer daters. As an accident waiting to happen with devastating results to good hearted people who may be victimized hoping to fall in love with a soul mate.

Love and Aging

What happens to your love as you age into a senior? In my case my admiration and respect for my wife increased each year. My wife was a Seven Day Adventist (SDA). Church members followed the Old Testament bible's guidelines scrupulously. No smoking, no drinking, no jewelry, the Sabbath was on Saturday, no unclean foods such as pork or fish without scales and who knows what else? Anna was an expert on the bible so much so that I was somewhat ashamed that I didn't know more about the bible. Anna went way out of her way to help people less fortunate than herself and anyone down on their luck. Anna had the humblest of origins and readily empathized and sympathized with their plight.

Anna loved animals of all types. You can't fool a cat. Over the years all of our cats liked Anna. Our latest cat, Cutie Pie, felt safe and comfortable in her presence. Cutie Pie would jump up on the bed and curl up next to Anna knowing that she would be safe and loved in Anna's presence. Cutie Pie was wary of strangers. Evidently animals possess a sixth sense regarding their welfare. I never met anyone who didn't come to like Anna. As I became older my admiration and respect for her grew. I liked holding Anna's hand. I never tired of it and was never ashamed displaying my affection for her. I could never understand couples feuding. I cannot recall an argument with Anna. There was no need for one. Since we were one in marriage why would I argue with myself? More often than not daily homelife was peaceful and I enjoyed going and being home. I was at home at home.

Love grew stronger as my wife and I grew older. Love was not the same it was as when Anna and I first married but, in many ways, while somewhat different our love was better. We were lucky since we both chose the right soul mate, the best decision that I ever made.

Repeated Reasons, Motivators and Goals in the Profiles of Women

In the search for happiness, few people want to go through life alone. Sample comments by women were:

- I want to grow old with someone. I want someone to complement me. I'd like someone to have my back when I'm down. I want someone to share my joy during happy times. Sharing my joy is so much better, almost magnified.
- I want someone to show me some affection often in private and on occasion in public.
- When we are old, I want to walk down the street hand in hand with my husband.
- I'm low maintenance. I'm not looking for wealth. I'd like to be treated like a lady with kindness, love and respect.
- I'd like to find a man that is polite, gentle and kind and treats me like the lady that I am.
- I want a man that is honest, loyal and does not lie to me or cheat.
- I'd like to marry a man with similar interests so that we can do things together.
- I want a man to teach me new things and increase my experiences.
- I want a man who is stable emotionally, physically, financially and mentally fit and a wonderful lover.
- I want a man who likes to travel so that we may experience new places together.
- Looking for a man who is an animal lover and likes my animals.
- I want my future husband to like children.
- I'd like my husband to be gentle, kind, not cheap and likes to travel together with me.
- I want my future mate to have a job, work hard and steady with a plan, a goal or goals.
- My husband should have a religion and go to church with me.

Women on Computer Dating

Following my wife's death, after 57 years of a happy marriage, I was lost living by myself. In a word, I became lonely. Marriage was a blessing. Anna and I had each other to talk to, confide in, to rely on, to be friends and to admire, respect and love. All that was gone with Anna's passing. We had had no children. After Anna's passing our house was essentially deserted, except for my cat, Cutie Pie, but my cat could not talk to me. I almost never received a telephone call from anyone that I wanted to talk to. Most of the telephone calls were sales calls and at my age, 82 I did not need or want anything, other than the basics which included food, I did not consider myself overly materialistic. In fact, as a senior I thought long and hard about downsizing and reducing the clutter that had accumulated over the years. I had no use for most of my wife's possessions, most of which went to Goodwill. I hired two people to help with the downsizing. After about two weeks we had progressed about as far as we could go sensibly because the easy work went quickly and was finished. As with the law of diminishing returns further decluttering would take a long time with very little visible progress.

Most of the time my house was eerily silent. I don't mind silence but not all the time. Of course, Cutie Pie didn't talk, and I was not a ventriloquist. It didn't take long for it to dawn on me that I was becoming lonely. My loneliness persisted and did not diminish. In fact, it increased in intensity. I was conflicted, I wanted to pay respect to my late wife's memory because she had been the best thing that ever happened to me. Anna had been the primary reason for my existence. I was dedicated to making her life better. I wanted her to be happy. That was my goal until the Alzheimer's ailment claimed her at 78. We had 57 years of a good life, love and happiness. All that was over, gone forever. Was I greedy, self-centered and an egotist consumed by my loneliness? Yet, I sulked about feeling sorry for myself and I did not want to feel sorry for myself. I had remembered reading somewhere that in order to take my mind off myself I needed to help someone else who needed help. I really didn't know many people since I retired 25 years ago. Most of my friends had passed away over the years. In short, I could not easily find anyone to help. As a result, I moped around becoming depressed, lacking a purpose and increasingly feeling sorry for myself while denying it. At this time my neighbor and current best friend Ted wandered by. Ted was very smart; he lived in the next apartment. Ted is black and a bachelor. I told Ted of my plight. Ted knew and always liked Anna. They spoke to each other frequently. Ted knew that I had loved my wife and that we had been happily married. I told Ted that I was feeling down in the dumps and he proposed that I avail myself of a computer dating service that he had had some success with. Ted thought that it may be the solution to my woes. Ted felt sorry for me and wanted to help me. He must have read that help book too.

I tried Ted's suggestion and wondered if I could find an eligible caring lady. I was 82 and I had a stroke in 2015. I was getting around slowly on a walker which made dating more complicated. My search for a wonderful lady companion is a work in progress to end when my goal is achieved.

To begin with I was curious about what type of women availed themselves on the computer dating service. Since I was trying computer dating perhaps other men may feel the same as I did. At this juncture, I have at long last arrived at the topic at hand, that is women on the computer dating service. Take a seat if you are not sitting already. You are in for abuse and punishment. What else did you expect, this isn't rocket science is it?

Profiles in General

Repeating myself ad nauseum I have read hundreds of profiles of women on the computer dating service. Again, the profile is the name of the mechanism/vehicle by which men and women describe themselves in detail and their desires for a person of the opposite sex. Each candidate completes answers to a series of defining questions. When completed in detail others will be able to determine if the information and photographs included provide the necessary information to describe desirable, in my case, women. At the end of each lady described the potential dating candidate may be contacted by typing her a message with your interest and honorable intentions related to further communications to allow her to determine face to face if there is any spark or mutual attraction. That outcome would help to determine if the parties had some hope for pursuing the relationship to the next level with the idealistic ultimate goal of marriage. Many ladies indicate that they do not want to get serious about marriage. What they want is dating and companionship and to see where companionship leads to if at all. In some instances, a woman specifies up front that she wants to become married as a result of computer dating. I had been a recent widower and I was still grieving out of respect for my late wife's memory. I did not want to remarry too quickly if I marry at all. Additionally, if the lady is anxious to marry quickly will she really love me or be consumed with her desire to be married? If I'm 82 and the lady who wants to marry is in her seventies how long would it take for one of us to go to the happy hunting ground (expire) and then back to square one?

The next topic ruffled the feathers of my wonderful computer helper and she took exception to my logic. My wife and I were broke when we married. Over years of work she and I amassed some money. I felt badly that I could not spend it all on her, but she was not overly interested in wealth. Anna was concerned with helping people less fortunate, that is why I'm hoping that she is in heaven. I am reminded of an old Henny Youngman joke. He said, "I told my wife that everything we owned belonged to her: the bank account, the cars, the house, everything. When I came home from work the next day, I found out that she had sold our house."

If at 82 I marry a lady in her seventies, and I pass away the next day she inherits all of my and my late wife's savings. What about my remaining relatives and the many charities that I liked, particularly animal related charities? This logic did not sit well with Christine (computer lady) but I can't help it. I suppose if I really loved the new older bride madly or if I hated my family or relatives I would not care.

Of course, if I am dead what happens will be beyond any concern of mine, oh well.

I have now arrived. The ladies on the computer dating service for the most part, are surprisingly beautiful, this includes the black ladies. The service has a section entitled: "Wants to Meet You." I was surprised that several black women wanted to meet me. Was this a mistake? While surprised I was flattered as well. I had to gulp or swallow because these women were unbelievably attractive. I had a photograph of myself in the dating service, but I could not believe a black lady was interested in me. Am I normal or a racist for not pursuing any of the inquiries but I was busy pursuing others and I left the beautiful black ladies for Ted my neighbor as if I made a difference or if I influenced anyone by my decisions? I say this in jest, but I remember Oscar Wilde's memorable quote: "I can resist anything but temptation." My motives are pure but as a Catholic I could always go to confession to absolve my sins.

Moving right along, in case you forgot, previewing profiles of lovely ladies beats crossword puzzles, Sudoku and poker. It is addictive. Besides being beautiful, most of the ladies are college graduates. Surprisingly many of the women had doctorate degrees and post doctorate achievements. From my experience doctorates are not handed out willy nilly. You have to be very smart and an expert in your field of expertise. I was not smart enough to be a Doctor of Mechanical Engineering. Many other professions are just as difficult. My hat is off to any doctor and I respect the level of intelligence needed. Perhaps doctorate standards were lowered but I seriously doubt it. I think people are smarter, especially women. As more and more opportunities are available to them since women have always been smart, we, this country, need as many people with doctorates as possible to stay competitive. I understand that most of the college students today are women. Maybe I can marry a rich lady who did not inherit it from her late husband, although it wouldn't matter to me. This reminds me of Groucho Marx who told Margaret Dumont "I would love you just as much if you had eight million dollars as when you had ten million dollars."

Many of the profiles of women are extremely well written reflecting an excellent and intelligent mind. I don't know if I could marry a woman a lot smarter than me. I wonder if she had neglected basic skills such as cooking, sewing and whatever is needed to maintain an efficient home. Of course, I could always hire a chef and a maid and whoever else was needed.

While I'm at it I have to identify a problem. If you received a "D" in English skip the comments. Many ladies confused compliment and complement. Compliment is saying something nice about anyone or anything. Complement is making something whole or better by being together. A wife may be good at taxes and a husband could be good at carpentry or car repairs. The partners complement each other. Although my example could be better but I'm not Noah Webster. But you know that despite this knit picking criticism, I mean well. The quality of the writing by the ladies on the computer dating service was exceptional and a joy to read. I'm stopping this portion of this essay on a high note, otherwise I may be chased out of town, but I could use the exercise, especially on a walker.

RELIGION AND COMPUTER DATING WOMEN

Many women do not list any religion or religious preference on their profile. Many women list a religion from Catholic, the most popular to an occasional Hindu, Buddhist or Muslim. Often women expressed the desire that their date go to church or pray with them or read the Bible together. They let it be known that religion and God play an important part in their daily existence. Some men will not date a woman with a religion not the same as his. Most didn't complain about it.

I do not object to marrying a woman who is not a Catholic. She may be Baptist, Jewish, Presbyterian, Methodist, Christian, other, or non-religious. Catholics and Baptists predominated. I believe there was a Hindu, a Buddhist and a Muslim. For my part I do not object to any religion and if married I would respect my partner's religion and attend church with her, at least occasionally. A woman has the right to go to heaven as she chooses. A surprising number of women were non-religious. No one put the word heathen or devout coward or the church the perpetual motion in their profile.

IS THE GLASS HALF FULL OR HALF EMPTY?

I discovered after reading women's profiles, more often than not, women are preoccupied with providing an opinion about whether a glass is half full or half empty. From my guess half empty implies pessimism, half full implies optimism. I gave it some though and I did not know the correct answer to the half full glass of water and decided not to linger on the issue. I think that I solved the enigma. What I would do is to put the entire contents of the half full glass so that it completely fills a smaller glass, problem solved; it's always full.

HONESTY IS A TWO-WAY STREET

Women insist that they want their men to be honest with them. My first profile omitted my stroke information. In my case what I have included is my revised "About Me" section, which is included in whole or partially for review. I added the fact that I had had a stroke in 2015 and that I was getting around with assistance on a walker. Many women insisted on honesty. I felt that I would be more transparent and honest by not omitting the stroke walker information. Secondarily, I was hoping that a few ladies would empathize similar to Clara Barton or Florence Nightingale and would come to my aid. However, no Clara or Florence were to be found no matter the size of any search party. In my case honesty was not the best policy when it came to locating a potential date or a companion, much less a friend, based on perceived honesty on my part. Honesty went by the wayside and did not help, so far.

BALLPOINT PENS (ADDED AS BONUS POINTS)

I have a box full of ballpoint pens. Most of these pens were free I'm guessing from a bank, motel or through advertisements mailed to me. I frequently receive a telephone call where I must record a telephone number, an appointment time, the location of a building or directions. At some point I have to reach for a ballpoint pen. More often than not I pick up a ballpoint pen that I cannot use to write anything. Is it out of ink, dry or unusable at the outset? To me the most reliable ballpoint pen is made by the Bic Corporation. I can buy a pack or container of Bic ballpoint pens really cheap at Walmart. These pens come in black, blue and red and what do you know; they write on the first try. The problem is that my Bic pens are never around when I want one, unlike imposters. Bic ballpoint pens have a talent for hiding when needed. Other ballpoint pens are very colorful on the exterior covered with advertising. The stems of Bic pens are transparent with a cap at one end. I am not proposing any solutions, resigned to the fact what can't be cured must be endured. No solution exists which leads to the classic comment, "If they could put a man on the moon, does he own a reliable ballpoint pen?"

The Use Of Attention In An "About You" Section of a Computer Dating Profile

Can you believe that the computer dating service had the following "About You" section in a woman's profile and I paraphrased it to tone it down a bit?

> My husband travels a great deal on his job. While he is away, I don't get enough attention from him. I am looking for someone to provide me with attention when my husband is away. When my husband is away for an extended period, I need an increased level of attention.

I love the English language. I love words, their meanings and how words may be manipulated to have any number of meanings. The use of the word *attention* in this instance is a far cry from its use in the Army. When I was in the Army there was no question of its meaning. It is the best use of attention since it is not specific, it covers a multitude of sins. In addition, it leaves to the reader to conjure up the meaning of attention. Is there a similar meaning that is any better? Perhaps covet from the Bible may approach its intent. If your mind is pure the meaning of attention is inoffensive. Complete the meaning and see the beauty of its latest meaning. This beauty of the English language is that the same word may have multiple meanings. Multiple meanings of a word complicate the language for foreigners or for the uninformed. Is it possible for someone complying with the lady's wishes be at attention and at ease simultaneously, similar to an oxymoron?

What Price Success?

When I started my quest for love at 82, I contacted women that appeared nice. Many women were too far away in New Jersey, New York City, Virginia and as far away as Utah. I was really attracted to the beautiful women in Utah, but my hopes were dashed summarily the distance made it all but impossible, especially with me using a walker.

After my first barrage of outreach I received three telephone replies. One beautiful Russian woman wanted 1,000 dollars to pay her rent which was due. She lived near Washington, D.C. I spoke to Ted, my neighbor and he suggested that since I did not know her, she may have been a scammer. I am gullible and a soft touch. I am empathetic since I say to myself "There but for the grace of God go I." When I told her that I had a spare bedroom she wanted to move in with her young daughter. I did not know this woman although her photograph was on my tablet and she appeared attractive to me, a lonely widower. I did not pursue her marital status. Our telephone conversation was amicable, portending compatibility. I had reservations about having someone to move in who was not my wife. Blame it on my religious upbringing. I hope that there is room in heaven for me. I want to join my late wife someday. That lead withered on the vine. I snatched defeat from the possibility of success.

My next setback occurred when I contacted a pretty nurse in Elkton, Maryland; a city close to me. The city where Babe Ruth was married and eventually disliked, following his divorce. Elkton was once considered the marriage capital of the East because the waiting time to become married was short. The nurse wrote that she wanted me to help pay her bills and she was working overtime in order to pay her bills. Don't nurses receive good wages? She said that if I paid her bills, she would have a social life and spend time with me. She wanted me to become her sugar daddy. This situation left a bad taste in my mouth; our first conversations concerned money. Will this woman love me for me or for my money? Would she love me if I was broke? Do I look like a pigeon; I've been called a dirty bird before, am I fulfilling a prophecy? There you have it my first two attempts at love that were shot down unceremoniously in flames. Better luck to you. I do not plan to throw in the towel. Either I am resilient or dumb. Don't answer that. I'd like to keep you posted on my progress but don't expect "Breaking News" from me. At the moment I feel more like the tortoise than the hare, but the quest isn't over yet. Maybe it is the beginning of a long arduous journey. I thought it would be easier.

Smoking, Alcohol Drinking, Exercise and Diet

Most of the women on the computer dating service were health and fitness conscious and reveal this in their "About You" section writeups. Women had a goal of eating healthful meals and working out in a gym several times weekly. These women seem to enjoy exercise and want their dates to join them doing their workout in the gym. The ladies enjoy walking often; some walk many miles daily. If not walking, biking will do. It is not unusual for women to proudly include, "I am physically fit, and I try to eat healthy food." At present frequent and long walks and exercise eliminates me as a potential date. No wonder it is difficult for me to find a date based on their profile preferences.

For my circumstances it is better for a woman to review my profile and select me but that hasn't happened to date (no pun intended). I admire anyone over 90 years old who brags, "I never exercised a day in my life." I met one.

For their first date many ladies want to go to a quiet spot for a cup of coffee or a glass of wine. A majority of women indicate that they are not a drinker of alcohol and nearly all of them were non-smokers. Women liked to visit wineries and drink microbrewery beers. Interestingly one middle aged, very attractive woman smoked cigars and there was a photograph of her puffing on one. I distinctly remember kissing a woman who smoked; it left an unpleasant taste in my mouth not a minty fresh taste. I prefer a non-smoker, but quitting smoking is no easy task for many. I had been a smoker for years. I would like to add that the smoke permeates a person's clothes. Non smokers may detect smoke odor in a date's clothes. Not to mince words a blunt crude date could say, "You stink." It is that bad to a non-smoker.

It was not unusual for my wife to cook with garlic in many meals. I liked it. One woman that I worked with could detect the smell of garlic odor; was she part bloodhound? As soon as I entered a room she would shout "You've been eating garlic again, haven't you?" I like garlic occasionally. It is healthful and no one ever died of garlic poisoning. I read that no other animal eats garlic. This useful information could allow you to win a trivia contest; that is about it.

Telephone Dating (Somewhat Redundant About Me)

After 57 years of a happy marriage I am a recent widower; a condition that I dislike. I am sociable and I'd like someone who likes me to talk to me often. With no children at home it's me, my cat, 'Cutie Pie' and three outside black strays, the TV and the telephone; which reminds me that my car's warranty has expired. At 82 I am computer challenged and at best type hunt and peck 10 words per minute. I have five self-published books; four of which are joke books. You may Google my books under my name, Alex Gall. I delegated all my book typing to others for a fee.

After 32 years I am a retired supervisory engineer and supervised up to 10 test technicians and test engineers for 28 years. Following a stroke in 2015 I am on a walker. Dancing and long walks are out for me, out of necessity, sorry. I took Arthur Murray lessons and jogged for years; but that's life. I am a very tolerant Catholic and a hazel-eyed Scorpio. Here's a sample of a joke from one of the books: If Federal Express merged with United Parcel Service would the new company be called Fed-Up? My jokes are creative, clean, original and often funny, you doubt me?

Judge me by my background and work. Ladies, if interested contact me. It is easier if you are truly interested in me. I was advised not to give out my phone number, but I'd really like to provide it, that's me. What a world! Sorry I am too trusting. I passed the Army written test and speak broken Hungarian along with Bela Lugosi. Bela, my middle name is William in Hungarian for anyone dying to know.

I am a one-woman guy and loyal by choice as if I could have been a Don Juan, fat chance. I'd like a religious woman who is non-smoking, drug free with minimal alcohol use. I have been completely faithful. I did not want to make comparisons. I am easy going and not pretentious. My second language is Hungarian. I prefer ladies 25 or older. I am a hazel-eyed Scorpio. I don't travel often. At 82 my mind is still sharp. I read many aspirations of lovely ladies. Those who truly like me with my candid strengths and weaknesses are attracted to me at the outset. Otherwise pursuing others is somewhat unproductive and I may be wasting precious time. If you don't like me, I'm a dead duck. That's it in my experience. I am a great conversationalist and story teller.

A Few Memorable "About Me" Remarks

I cannot in good conscience include all comments that some women made in the "About Me" profile section since comments could be considered obscene. I struggled with a few that I included. I didn't want to burn in hell.

- If you are here for a hook up keep moving.
- Times goes by in the blink of an eye.
- If you want to play games shop at Toys R Us.
- Black woman: I believe in over the top passion and love as I have had it in the past and look forward to experiencing it again and possibly better the second time again.

Me after reading the aforementioned: Hmmm, what would I do? I'm a lonely widower and not a racist. I'd do what I usually do – nothing.

- First off, my name is . . . and I don't date outside of my race.
- I don't date black men.

Random Comments in the "About Me" Section of Profiles

To save time I made it a point not to fail to read all of the profiles that I could. I concentrated on eligible women who appeared to have similar interests as I had. How closely did we think alike? Many women put up barriers such as, "If you voted for Donald Trump pass me by. If you're not between 40 and 60 keep moving. If you are too young, I'm not interested. If you are not at least six feet tall we may not be suited since I am a tall woman. If you have a beard (ugh)."

To attract a man, women would tout their education. A surprising number had master's degrees or even a doctorate. Many ladies stated that they were self-sufficient, could support themselves, low maintenance, humorous, witty, easy to get along with, a pleasant disposition and much, much more and it did not end there, it began there. The more profiles that I read the more I wanted to read even more. Knowledge is power. Not only were they revelatory they were unquestionably interesting, in style and charm on occasion brilliant in content, honesty and eloquence. It came to the point that I scrutinized each profile primarily zeroing in on the "About Me" portion of the profile. Some

"About Me" sections were so excellent and candid in its content that I developed an immediate liking and admiration for the woman, and it would not take too much effort to begin to fall in love with a woman of her caliber. Was she shot out of a cannon; she had the proper caliber? By contrast disappointingly many "About Me" areas were blank. Was the woman lazy, poor in basic English and writing or not serious about love? The "About Me" sections became habit forming a bell weather. I read "About Me" first not reading specific individual profile details. Why would a woman decide to omit the "About Me" write-up? One woman wrote, "No one reads this section anyway. Why fill it out?" Well, excuse me!!! What galls me, and again I use that word loosely, her opinion was the opposite of mine.

Several white women, especially older women, stated "I don't date black men" or commented about not dating out of their race. When a woman expressed a strong desire for a man of a different race I began to think, is it possible that youthful experiments or experiences became imprinted on a person's brain and those first experiences carry into adulthood and are accepted as normal love relationships? I have seen this phenomenon in my own limited travels. "As the twig is bent so grows the tree."

One black woman said eloquently in her profile and I paraphrase, "I'm not afraid to date out of my race because I think people are beautiful regardless of race color no matter what." The profiles did not dwell on interracial dating. It wasn't too much or too little, but the profiles reflected reality and did not ignore or duck the issue which added to its unbiased realism and balance. The issue was not swept under the rug.

My Dating Profile

After 57 years of marriage I am a recent widower, a condition that I dislike. I am sociable and I'd like to talk to a woman who likes me. At present it is just me and my cat, Cutie Pie, the TV and the telephone telling me that my car's warranty has expired. I am computer challenged and hunt and peck 10 words a minute, tops. I have five self-published books; four joke books, that you can Google under my name. Typing the books was delegated to others for a fee.

I am a retired supervisory engineer for 28 years supervising up to 10 test engineers and test technicians at Aberdeen Proving Ground, MD. Following a stroke in 2015 I've been on a walker. While my brain is sharp, I have limited mobility so dancing and long walks are out, of necessity, sorry. I was an Arthur Murray student as well as a jogger for decades but that's history.

I am a tolerant Catholic and a hazel-eyed Scorpio. Hungarian is a second language. I love old gypsy music that I heard in my youth. I passed the Army written test in Hungarian and I speak it passably, but not intellectually. I was not schooled in Hungarian. I'm self-taught by understanding their alphabet and knowing the language. I prefer women within a 20-mile radius of Havre de Grace, MD. It's easier. I am somewhat of a homebody now. I love to read, watch TV and listen to the radio. I am a one-woman guy, creative, almost honest and loyal. I am a great conversationalist with a wonderful wit, sense of humor and modest.

I prefer a religious woman who is a non-smoker, no drugs (other than prescription) and with moderate alcohol use. After reading hundreds of interesting, wonderful profiles and requirements of lovely women seeking eligible men I concluded that it would be better to list my strengths, limitations and desires, rather than try to select a woman based on her perceived desires and needs. If a woman still likes me after considering my strengths and limitations my search is dramatically reduced. I hope that my approach proves to be fruitful. I'm short of fruit, come to think of it. If interested contact me. It's easier for me. Although I love to write, I type poorly.

I'd like to meet someone humble and unpretentious to visit me regularly as a good platonic friend. At my age hugs and kisses go a long way avoiding the need for a pacemaker. A regular date may not be in the cards, but the spirit is willing.

The Statue of Liberty loves me. She told me that she's been carrying the torch for me for years. My original humor is quick and hard to beat. Read my four joke books, you will agree.

Profiles and "About Me" Revisited

In the computer dating service as stated, the profile provides pertinent information defining an individual, everything from height, age, hair color, eye color, marital status, etc. Within the profile is a section entitled "About Me". The "About Me" section allows each candidate an opportunity to help define a candidate's personality, character, humor, views, honesty, philosophy and anything that a candidate deems important or anything he or she would like a future date or an eventual mate to know. The information provided in the "About Me" section may be factual or more often than not opinions, feelings, philosophies, inclinations, beliefs, life lessons that may be less factual and more emotional in nature. Once I scan the factual data I go directly to the "About Me" section to assess a candidate's logic, beliefs, values, or philosophy. Many people do not contribute to the "About Me" section to my disappointment because I get the impression that I'm lacking useful information. If a woman hates President Trump, I would like to know that. Especially if she will not date or get along with someone who voted for President Trump.

I have included my "About Me" section of my profile. I do not want to plagiarize someone else's "About Me" section. If I repeat parts of my "About Me" often perhaps it may help you to remember it easier.

Discussing the "About Me" Section of Women's Profiles

Some memorable comments in the "About Me" section of specific profiles come to mind. There are many more, but I need to refresh my memory, review many profiles and collect my thoughts. This exercise was time consuming. Have I lied to you before or shouldn't I ask that question again? Music is life. "A smiling face, a warm embrace, it's time to find the person who cares that I wake up. I wear boots specifically to walk through your BS. If you are married, in a complicated relationship, bi-sexual, cross dresser, into sin or 50 Shades of Grey or 20 shades of paint pass me by."

The following quotations were extracted from women's profiles. They are often memorable and reflect the diversity of comments. Many quotes are surprisingly unorthodox and refreshing besides being entertaining.

1. If you are weird in any way, shape or form and looking for a hook-up please move on.
2. If you think you are going to catfish me, think again.
3. If you want to talk about just boobs and sex keep looking.
4. Can't have any tattoos. I don't like motorcycles either.
5. I like to go to the junk yard and work on an old car.
6. Bob, if you are still there you were so right.
7. The older I get the bigger my list of quirks seem to get but I promise you to know me is to tolerate me.
8. The point is it's nice to have someone to talk to that you didn't give birth to.
9. But it's nice to vary it up sometimes and have an adult conversation with someone who doesn't share your DNA.
10. Hitting the elevator button 10X isn't going to make it come back any faster.
11. I don't speak Pig Latin nor deal with swine so don't kid me, no beard/move.
12. I'd like to build a fence around your heart not a wall.
13. And yet just a quiet time at home is best shared.
14. Say what you mean and mean what you say. I'm not here with my ass or my hand out Plus.
15. Stop asking me what I do because if I wanted to tell you my occupation it would be listed.
16. Trying to be scammer free zone. My BS radar is very sensitive.
17. Looking for my partner in crime. Come let's set the world on fire.

18. I am attracted to confidence although arrogance is a turn off.
19. If you are addicted to your phone, I'm not the woman for you.
20. No, I didn't vote for Trump and I can't see any successful relationship with someone who supports him or his agenda.
21. Also don't message me for money; I'm not a cash machine.
22. Remember your appearance on the outside fades but the heart is what I'm interested in.
23. One-night flings go elsewhere; that's not me.
24. Don't message me if you're a dumbo.
25. If you use a word incorrectly, I have to process it in my head first or I can't process the rest of the conversation.
26. I prefer simple genuine and low key versus flash and bling.
27. No one reads this anyway so why bother to fill it out?
28. So let the music play, let's dance and be merry. The night is young, and they are playing our song.
29. I don't like to play games unless it's Monopoly.
30. I don't have time for needy men, unstable men, selfish men.
31. I'm a firm believer in that life is selfless and that's how we should live them.
32. If you are going overseas, please don't contact me.
33. I like dating handsome black men. If you are a white male I will not respond. I'm only interested in my black kin.
34. Not here to talk about my boobs.
35. Don't play games and not hooking up with anyone.
36. No separated, married, girlfriend, bisexual.
37. If you are ages 20 to 30 don't bother.
38. Honesty is an absolute must. I have five kids.
39. I'm looking for a man who can afford to take me to lunch.
40. If you tell me you're in the military – currently overseas and you are looking for your soulmate on here, odds are you are fake so don't waste my time.

Alex Gall

Sweat the Small Stuff

Details are critical to accomplish computer dating successfully. Attention to detail will avoid or minimize problems later. It is desirable to locate a potential date close to your residence. I would like to see a date often to get to know her better. Distance in dating is an enemy. In bad weather a 20-mile drive can stop a romance cold. A telephone call is no substitute for hugs and kisses.

Tall women are somewhat reluctant to date short men and remind future daters of this fact which may be psychological and subconscious. Same height couples see eye to eye. With a taller woman the man looks up to her. With a taller man the woman may look up to him.

Age differences may be a barrier. I don't mind dating a young woman unless she looked to be my daughter or niece. Some women would not like their date to look younger or he may be mistaken as her son, cousin or nephew. No one wans to hear the word pedophile to come up in conversation or thought of seriously. If a date wants to be married and announces it, it may be better to date someone for companionship first. It is best to date someone you are comfortable with regard to profession or education. A high school drop out and a college professor or a doctorate may not be a good match or even good company.

Some dates do not speak English. Their profiles may be entirely in Spanish. Date people who speak your language. If your date has ten children it may prove to be a problem, who watches the children? How much privacy will there be? How about the noise level? It is well to remember that the safety and welfare of children, grandchildren and great grandchildren are the first order of business, your primary concern, never to be forgotten. While you're at it how about pets regarding feeding, safety and keeping an eye on them? No one wants to lose a pet or have one hurt.

You may want to date a slender or full-figured person, double check the photograph, don't leave it to others. Be aware of a date's tendency to drink or smoke. Many people cannot tolerate smokers at any level. Several religions frown on the use of alcohol. It is easier to avoid alcohol beforehand than to stop it once started. It is best to date someone with the same or similar religions. A quick look at profile information may prevent or minimize religious misunderstandings. I don't want to name any specific religions in order to avoid any unwarranted offense or criticism.

Be certain that transportation is available. Does one party own or rent a car or in a large city is a bus or taxi best? If ethnicity may prove to be an issue this can be determined easily. Besides African American and Caucasian, the two most listed, there are many mixed designations clouding ethnicity. Do you want to date someone with children? Is there one child involved or ten? If you are single you may have a hard time adjusting to the increased noise level, the overall lack of privacy or the increased levels of demands and services required such as school or doctor visits.

Be sure to determine if your date is not still involved with a former girlfriend, wife, friend, a separation or a widow. Past relationships could be undesirable if comparisons are made to past and present associations. Past relationship feelings may still linger to interfere with the development of a new romance, the progress of love.

Read the entire profile and especially the About Me portion. There are often reservations and prohibitions scattered throughout the profile provided. Ignoring prohibitions could invite grief later. Again, be sure you check all photographs very carefully. You may find tattoos, piercings, undesirable amorous friends, previous dates or embarrassing situations. Your future date may be in a photograph at an outing or a party where she is surrounded by early life forms, goons, aliens or items that you object to based on your religion merely as one example I have no idea what people find offensive.

In the Army there was an expression "To be forewarned is to be forearmed." Or Franklin's phrase, "An ounce of prevention is worth a pound of cure."

I repeat, it is essential to review all of the photographs of potential dates. Many women are strikingly beautiful, but danger lurks when least expected. A lovely lady could call herself a "beach bum". Guess what folks, I just married a bum. Or several women characterized themselves as class clowns. Guess what folks I dumped the bum and married a clown. Candidates must be evaluated in totality considering pertinent pros and cons before making a final decision.

Most of the women in a large population are average looking and not amazingly beautiful. I study a woman's face and say to myself "She's very nice. I bet I could get along with her and learn to love her she has so many other exemplary wifely qualities.

Some women cannot cook or don't want to and brag that they have a talent for locating desirable restaurants every day. Therefore, every day I would be driving all over town looking for parking somewhere and waiting for a tasty meal. Other good looking women confess they can't or don't like to cook and expect a husband to cook it all or assist in the kitchen. Do I want a beautiful woman who can't or dislikes cooking or a less attractive woman who is a good cook and still a loving wife? Don't forget your children eat too and need regular meals. If you get lucky you could date and marry a beautiful chef, but don't hold your breath.

It is that simple. I wanted to share the elements that triggered that feeling of joy, peace and contentment that I could identify in hindsight and never thought about because they were not apparent when they occurred. Perhaps unknown to my wife, as well. Rather than dwell on negatives I prefer to accentuate the positives. Why be mired in anguish longing, grief, broken promises, dreams, struggles, doubt, crying, impatience, disappointments which do not further the pact of love? I prefer to list Anna's positive actions, attributes and habits that made every day better little by little adding to my joy, contentment and peace of mind.

The following is a partial list of Anna's positive attributes. There are many more.

- Happy disposition
- Joy
- Love of animals
- Laughing at my jokes
- Love for me
- Enthusiasm
- Cheerfulness
- Happiness
- Concern for my welfare
- Her encouragement
- Her belief in me
- Her mere presence

- Speech
- Smile
- Doing nice little things for me
- Hugs and kisses
- Cooperation
- Agreeable disposition
- Candor and honesty
- Concern for others
- Her religiousness and basic goodness
- Her belief in God and the afterlife
- Belief in her salvation
- Beauty and loveliness
- Lively spirit
- Respect for life – people and animals
- Friendship
- There you have it, there are many more.

SUCCESS – AT LONG LAST

How will you know when all of your efforts looking for love at any age has proven to be successful? You will not get a bronze, silver or gold medal no my friend. Congratulations you are near the last chapter of this book. You are classified by me into one of two groups.

1. Totally out of luck, even a visually impaired squirrel will find an acorn once in a while. Luck has a lot to do with dating and you may be down on your luck or unlucky in love. That's the breaks. Conditions could change quickly, and you may need a club to beat off dates especially if you were the last men on earth. Remember everyone has a talent. Dating may not be your talent.
2. The second group of readers may have had limited success with several dates. Dates that ran hot and cold, off and on, now and then but no real pay dirt just flashes in the pan. No knight in shinning armor or soulmate, no current squeezes, princesses, no Cinderella, no love of your life. You are still searching, you've met Mr. or Ms. Wrong but no Mr. or Ms. Right for you. You are still unfulfilled, not at peace, not confident with your lot

and circumstances, still yearning for that missing something that elusive pot of gold at the end of the rainbow.

I went back and reviewed the tribute to my late wife, Anna. I was happy and content with what I wrote but in retrospect was it all there or was something missing, something that I had forgotten? One night it dawned on me. What was it as a happily, married man that made me happy? No one thing made me happy, it was not as if I had crossed a finish line. It was the sum of a lot of little things similar to building a house one brick at a time.

I thought of all of the little things that Anna did that pleased me. I decided to list these small positive building blocks to my happiness which may trigger your recognition of them when and if similar events or feelings are recognized by you when and if it or whatever it is that they appear in your life and marriage. In my case happiness was the ultimate goal of my search for love.

I want everyone to know in their travels and quest for love how will you know that you have arrived at your goal your destination; that you have found love? Anna's positive attributes that added to my happiness was summarized and explained when required. These positive attributes are not listed in any specific order for this reason. I think of ordering an ice cream sundae, it is delivered and looks good yet there is something missing. It is not perfect. Then I ask, where is the cherry on the top, it is not perfect?" I'm missing one cherry; the smallest most insignificant element yet it is the difference between being happy and being ecstatically happy. Don't ask me to explain it. I cannot. Is life just a bowl of cherries, after all?

Love Your Spouse

I've hoped that I have saved the most important message for last. Once you have found your true love, your knight in shinning armor, your soulmate who remains to be the very person that was the most important thing in your life, your reason for living, your inspiration, the primary reason for your joy, peace of mind, your contentment, your reason for working? Your spouse is the mother or father of your children, your living legacy.

Do not forget to tell your spouse as often as you can how much you love him or her. What does it cost you? Tell your wife that she is the best thing that ever happened to you. Tell her that you will never leave her and that she has made your life worthwhile. Remind her often that you would jump at the chance to marry her again since no one could ask for a better wife. Tell your wife that your life, your happiness began when you married her. Let her know that you have been completely faithful and that you took your marriage vows seriously and that you will never leave her until death do you part. Ask her if she needs anything including money for something that she would like to have or may need.

How would you feel if your wife passed away suddenly and you have not made her feel better by not telling her how much that you loved her and how wonderful a wife that she has been? You only go around once, you cannot get back again. Take the opportunity to tell your wife just how much you love her and how happy that she had made you over the years. You will be glad that you did; in this life and perhaps the next.

Final Thoughts

Good luck on your quest for love. I hope you get lucky and find what you are looking for quickly. In my case after Anna's passing, I had many problems with little hope of success. A few women who I met were defensive. I had to be careful not to say anything that could be misunderstood. I hadn't thought that what I said was offensive. It may have been an inferiority complex or insane jealousy. For my part I did not like seeing my date with an old flame. I was jealous. In some cases, I found out later that my date's friends were her sons or cousins and I had jumped to an incorrect undesirable conclusion essentially triggering jealousy or an aversion. Things are never quite as simple as it seems. Everything seems to take longer to achieve. While dating I don't like sharing a date with another suitor; is this normal? It is for me; maybe I'm greedy, I prefer monogamy.

At present my life is less happy since my wife died. I can't seem to attract another wonderful lady to date or talk to. I thought it would be easier. It is difficult for people to change a location or way of life quickly, similar to a large ship trying to change course. I am by nature impatient which is often undesirable. Perhaps I could meet an impatient woman. I am hoping something good will happen when I least expect it. So far, no woman has pursued me; that would be ideal. I remain optimistic but I want God to hurry; however, my problems must seem small in God's eyes.

The pursuit of love is similar whether you are 20, 30, 40 or 80 or more. The participants differ but the ultimate goal is a bond, happiness, a better life where two people complement each other and face their futures with confidence, resolve, optimism and hope ultimately to perpetuate the species and a myriad of other lesser goals.

To My Late Wife, Anna Gall a Tribute
Goodbye Anna, Anna Goodbye but not Forgotten

Background

My late wife Anna escaped from Hungary in 1956 during the Hungarian Revolution. She fled to the United States with her older brother, Joseph, who was to be drafted and sent to Siberia with other Hungarians, many of whom in the past it was rumored to have disappeared from there never to be seen or heard from again.

After leaving Hungary it was not certain as to which country would welcome Anna and Joe. Refugees were being scattered around the world like seeds. Luckily Anna and Joe ended up in the United States with Anna in New Jersey and Joe in Illinois.

To my good fortune Anna's path and my path crossed in the unlikely place called Garwood, New Jersey which is in roughly central

New Jersey, perhaps 30 miles west of New York City. In Garwood Anna lived in a spare bedroom in the house of an elderly Hungarian couple. During the day Anna worked in a small manufacturing plant that made plastic bottles.

I was attracted to Anna the moment that I saw her. Her colorful appearance and Hungarian accent were decidedly different. I never thought much about getting married since I was for all intents and purposes constantly broke, what with attending and paying for college and minimal income for six years during and after high school. I had worked for four years at the Westinghouse Corporation. I cannot believe it but the Westinghouse Corporation, an enterprise that I had admired and loved is no longer in existence. What caused its demise is a mystery to me, but it is a sad chapter in the annals of USA business. I worked at Westinghouse for the better part of the period that I attended four years of evening classes at the Newark College of Engineering (NCE). I graduated in 1961 with a Mechanical Engineering degree that was heavily weighted with industrial engineering/management courses. NCE was transitioning to an industrial engineering degree and these courses better suited my skills and inclinations.

My military deferment for six years expired upon graduation in 1961. With the launching of the Russian Sputnik satellite engineering had been declared an essential pursuit to the defense of the country, hence the deferment which allowed me, as with many others, to delay the military draft until I graduated. I was drafted into the Army in the Fall of 1961 and was sent to Fort Dix, New Jersey for basic training. I completed basic training in freezing December.

You may think that I disliked the Army, au contraire my friend. I was mixed in with younger trainees, many of whom were volunteers. At 24 years of age I was considered a senior citizen. After years of study and wracking my brain, I enjoyed exercising, running around, marching, singing and learning about being an Army soldier. As with most soldiers at that time I griped and counted the days left until my discharge date. I must admit I was happy to fulfill my obligation to serve my country. In reality, while I groused about it openly, I was having fun and enjoying myself after college. Essentially it was a welcome departure from the discipline and stress of constant tests that I had experienced and endured for six long years. My main complaint was that I wanted to make a decent wage based on my BSME degree. I wanted to get married and join the workforce. In the Army at that time I started at 78 dollars a day, once a month, plus room and board.

I married while in the Army and the US government provided my wife and me extra money for being married plus an allotment for modest rent. My life began to improve. I was assigned to the Human Engineering Laboratory (HEL) at Aberdeen Proving Ground (APG), Maryland. I assisted experimental psychologists as a technical gopher, a happy assignment for me since I slept in a cinderblock building at night and I was not being shot at during the day. The psychologists at the Human Engineering Laboratory were a joy to work with and I could commute home many weekends to be with my wife and visit my parents and family.

Anna's Good Deeds

My wife performed many selfless acts. A few examples will illustrate:

1. Once a year her Seventh Day Adventist church hosted a Vacation Bible School for the young people. Anna made sure that the youngsters attended. She used her car to round up the students at their homes and transport them to and from the church until the bible classes were over.
2. Anna helped assemble and distribute food baskets at Thanksgiving and Christmas to needy families. The church's school children helped to collect the food. The volunteer fire department and police departments contributed food as well. Emergency food baskets were assembled as needed during the year.
3. Anna provided clothes and furniture free to needy people. The furniture and clothes had been donated to the church. As an aside excess furniture and clothes were donated to Goodwill or The Salvation Army.

4. My neighbor Lineer was sick one evening and he contacted my wife who drove him to the hospital emergency room while I slept. Lineer recalled this story at my wife's viewing.
5. Lineer's mother died of breast cancer. At Anna's viewing Lineer said that Anna became his surrogate mother for years, a fact that I had suspected. Lineer has been my neighbor for nearly 60 years. I could not get along without Lineer since my stroke in 2015. Besides, Lineer is very intelligent.
6. Anna helped many people in Harford and Cecil Counties. She knew the roads in those counties like the back of her hand. Despite her weaving and circuitous routes Anna unfailingly ended up at her destination which amazed me since I was lost.

When Anna and I were out together frequently people would approach us and remind Anna of how she had helped them years earlier. My wife recognized everyone even decades later. On many occasions people did not have enough money to pay their gas and electric bill. Through the Seventh Day Adventist pastor the gas and electric bills were paid. On most occasions Anna was approached first because those in need knew that my wife would find a way and besides, they trusted Anna to get the task done.

Unknown to me many of the good deeds performed by Anna are interred in her grave with Anna.

Justification

I wrote this essay in order that my wife's existence on this earth could be appreciated and known to others and to understand the treasure that she was Anna was not just another random leaf in the wind. If someone reads this tribute 10 or 1000 years from now my hope is that they will gain some understanding of the beauty of Anna's soul. I'm hoping that this tribute, and my books, will be timeless but I don't want to be presumptuous or unrealistic.

After writing the essay I thought of something that needed to be said to people who will have an Alzheimers victim in their family or in their presence. As Alzheimers progressed I tended to be overly judgmental when my wife did anything bizarre. It took me a while to realize and adjust to her deteriorating condition. I found Anna feeding our cats vegetarian refried beans, garbanzo beans and all manner of people food. The cats would not eat the people food and I had to pitch it all out, food that I looked forward to eating. Once I found Anna happily eating a can of cat food. I became alarmed and quickly admonished her. I failed to realize that Alzheimer's symptoms were confusing her normal thoughts. I was ashamed of myself for leaping to a conclusion without considering the progress of her Alzheimers malady. With an Alzheimers patient it is essential to attribute the patient's strange activities to the root cause of any unusual behavior and hold the patient blameless for irrational activities that would never have occurred under normal circumstances.

Alzheimers Ailment Discussion

Introduction complete, let's continue with my wonderful wife of 57 years. Saying wonderful sounds so glib. I must repeat this Henny Youngman or Rodney Dangerfield joke (Anna loved it as well). My wife and I were happy for 21 years and then we met. Or, my wife and I were married for 57 years, the happiest three years of my life.

Anna passed away in an assisted living hospice in Aberdeen, MD on 25 July 2019. She had suffered from the Alzheimers curse. Based on my readings and what I was told by my retired registered nurse sister and my registered pharmacist step-brother the Alzheimers condition continues to worsen. My best friend's wife died from Alzheimers and her step-daughter confirmed a grim, cruel and ignominious end.

I cannot prove it, but I suspect that the toxins in hair spray mist may have had, over the years, a negative effect on Anna's brain function as it related to cognitive performance. Anna loved working and after menial jobs she decided to become a beautician. She went to beauty school for about one year. Anna passed both the practical and written tests and eventually became the manager for her employer's beauty parlor. Anna was mechanically gifted and basically intelligent. While customers are exposed to hair spray mist once or twice a year, beauticians, especially managers, are exposed to hair spray mist many times per week, sometimes daily. My wife was a spirited, lively, optimistic person all of her life until Alzheimers claimed her. The ailment progressed until Anna was unable to make rational decisions, even the most elementary and rudimentary ones. In hospice she was eating the thick crayons that I bought for her. Luckily the nurse removed the crayons.

To determine if hairspray mist may be linked to beautician's Alzheimers a simple study is proposed. Select two same size groups of retirees:

1. Beauticians – including managers
2. Non-beauticians

Determine the number of Alzheimers patients in each group.

Compare the incidence of Alzheimers in each group. For comparison purposes the larger the groups the better. The data may be analyzed to determine if one group's incidence of Alzheimers is significantly higher.

I have digressed from my main topic but with the rapid increase in the number of Alzheimers patients and the increasing number of elderly people something needs to be done. I am upset and mad about losing my wife. Future elderly people will be shocked by the expense of monthly nursing home care which may leave people bankrupt or destitute with entire families and even generations impoverished.

There may be a link with certain hair sprays and Alzheimers and a number of studies of hair spray and Alzheimers would be desirable. The studies should be at the federal level since the government may end up shouldering nursing home, assisted living, hospice and other burgeoning elderly health care costs. Perhaps I am all wet in my theory but if someone else has a better theory let him or her speak up and propose it.

As Alzheimers progressed Anna had a tendency of falling. Anna fell several times within our house. On two occasions, at night, I could not lift her. I had been on a walker following a stroke in my sleep in 2015. On both occasions I called 911 and Anna was transported to the hospital for x-rays and an examination. On one occasion she had a broken hip or leg and required an operation and was sent to a nursing home. The nursing home cost about 20 thousand dollars a month but I did not like her care because she spent most of her time in a bed or in a wheelchair with very little monitoring.

I had Anna moved to an assisted living facility that I had visited three times beforehand and found it to be friendly and comfortable with caring personnel. The patients there who I spoke to liked the facility. Overall the assisted living facility seemed better suited to care for Anna because they checked up on her often which eased my mind because Anna wanted to walk unassisted. I didn't want her to fall again.

In the assisted living hospice Anna was asleep for longer and longer periods and it became more and more difficult for her to swallow. I was told that in her final night she experienced severe pain around her hip. Anna had had three back surgeries years before and it could be that these disruptive procedures had left long term negative consequences including growing pain. In hospice the goal was to make the patient comfortable. To ease her pain Anna was given an injection of morphine. The pain did not diminish, and Anna began to cry from the greater pain. The level of morphine administered was increased and Anna died. My step-brother and sister stated that too much morphine can contribute to respiratory failure. A physician had been contacted by the assisted living hospice nurses to direct the morphine dose strength needed.

In cases of Alzheimers the end is a choice between the lesser of several poor alternatives with no proper solution. I'd like to think that God made the final decision but what do I know as a wayward Catholic?

Afterthoughts

What do I miss the most with the passing of my wife Anna? Seemingly trivial thoughts come to mind. Anna loved animals. I would scour the mail and elsewhere for pictures of cute animals. She especially liked pictures of kittens, puppies and any animal including pigs with a cute face and floppy ears. I would cut out and save likeable animal pictures. I felt very rewarded when she gazed at my pictures and said, "Ahhh, how cute, how lovely, don't you just love them?" and I did.

I miss not being able to do small acts of kindness for my wife when she least expected them. Anna had no living relatives in the United States. Her older brother Joe had died of a heart problem. Anna's younger brother, Frank, in Hungary, committed suicide as a result of a tormented failed marriage. Her parents were gone, and she was survived by one widowed sister and two married sisters and their families in Hungary. I told Anna frequently that my primary purpose in life was to make her life better and to maximize her happiness since she had no nearby family and we had no children. I told her often that I was her family and that I would stick to her like glue and never leave her. I said that I was very glad and thankful that I had married her and that she was the best thing that ever happened to me. In one of my joke books I read to her the words in my book's dedication which said, "To my wife Anna words cannot do her justice." Of course, I told Anna that I loved her. My love affirmation is somewhat redundant, albeit true. Anna and I were married 57 years. What more proof of love is needed?

Additional Considerations

What is the proper length of time for grieving? Whenever I think of Anna I tear up. I tear up at the most Inopportune times, often embarrassing me a senior a seemingly mature citizen. I admit to being lonely. I feel ashamed of myself for desiring the presence and companionship of a caring female. But with no children, almost no friends and fewer and fewer remaining my living area is deserted with no sign of life other than the television, the cat and the occasional telephone call.

I had put the word out through my wife's Seven Day Adventist church and other sources that I would not feel offended meeting a religious, non-smoking, non-alcohol using woman. I tried to justify and rationalize my furtive search efforts by saying that Anna would have wanted me to be happy. All the while I feared that I will be punished by not honoring and respecting my wife's memory by not grieving for a longer period. Evidently my greedy self-indulgent subconscious nature was managing to emerge and overcome my Catholic religious teachings of what it takes to be a sin free person. Had the priests and nuns failed?

I may have to go to confession and pray for forgiveness for not honoring the dead long enough. Anna, while I pray, I don't pray enough, that I may be with you again. In Catholicism, according to Saint Francis of Assisi, that in order to attain eternal life I have to die. Paraphrasing Woody Allen, "When I die, I don't want to be around when that happens". I'd like to believe that there is a heaven, but sacrilegiously I can't prove it conclusively. If there is a heaven Anna most certainly will be there based on her exemplary life. I know of no one who did more to help people in need. No one will ever know the true extent of her concern for others. In testimonials at her viewing I learned that Anna may have had a secret second life driving around in her old Honda looking for and helping unsuspecting targets for her dedication to downtrodden people.

Anna, boldly assuming that you are in heaven, I hope that if you have some pull and if you managed to get there, save me a seat next to you. I can't think of anyone I'd rather spend time with in eternity other than you. Anna, I love you. I was blessed to be able to spend 57 happy years with you. I was at peace being in your presence. You made me a better human being by your example.

I must add that my wife was extremely proud to be an American citizen and she professed her feelings openly and often. In retrospect I have one regret which keeps troubling me. I always wanted Anna to die at home within familiar surroundings. In assisted living I visited Anna daily, rain or shine. Anna was always friendly, loving and upbeat. I never expected her to die suddenly and I had no sense of urgency in that regard. Anna's excessive sleeping did not disturb me unduly, difficulty swallowing did. But I thought starving to death would take weeks and she did not appear to be losing weight.

Sound asleep one morning there was a frantic pounding racket on my front door which awakened me from a sound sleep. I immediately suspected the worst and I was right. I wanted to be by my wife's side holding her hand and comforting her so that she may pass away peacefully. No such luck. I wanted to ease her passing to the other side with me by her side comforting her. I was too late now with no way to undo and correct it. The end came unexpectedly quickly. No best laid plans occurred, no one warned me. If the assisted living personnel did not mention death, experienced as they were with Alzheimers, how could I know? I questioned the move to hospice since as I knew hospice was a prelude to death, but no one contradicted my suspicions. I went along with hospice since two nurses would be present and more skilled care would be available.

At this juncture what can I do to ease my troubled conscience by not being at Anna's side in her last moments. I felt that comforting her was my, as her loving husband, responsibility. Sometimes good intentions are not enough to overcome cruel events. Please forgive me!

I know that I am not the first person to look at his wife's lifeless body lying in her casket. I was sad and mad at the same time. I said to myself, "Anna, what happened? I don't want to believe this. Now what?" Time may heal all wounds, but it certainly doesn't lessen the pain. When thinking about my wife I feel so unworthy. Did I do enough?

The ending of the western movie 'Shane' floods my mind with its eerie parallel. As Alan Ladd rides off at night wounded Brandon De Wilde, the youthful star, plaintively cries out. In Anna's case I wanted to shout, "Anna, come baaaccckkk. I want you. I need you, Annnnnnaaa!" Pardon me for crying, I can't help it, I'm grieving again. Reluctantly I telephoned Anna's sister Barbara in Hungary telling her of Anna's passing in my broken Americanized Hungarian. Barbara thanked me. After the funeral I sent a photo of Anna in her casket to Barbara, but the letter was in English. I did not feel comfortable writing in Hungarian since I am self-taught and no doubt inadequate in writing.

Goodbye Anna, I'll take your memory to my grave, where I'll be forgotten along with countless of others. I'm coming Anna, I hope to see you soon, if I'm lucky.

I can rest somewhat easier now that this tribute to Anna helps to relieve my troubled and remorseful brain. May your future be free from the scourge of the Alzheimers malady. Similar to a large whirlpool, not only is the patient caught up but anyone in its swirl is inexorably swept into its vortex.

Alex Gall

    I wanted to include this essay in my sixth book, but I am 82 years old and time may be of the essence. If I don't distribute the essay soon, I run a risk. I am no stranger to anonymity but being dead will take time to get used to.

PLUS (ESSAYS)

Is It Charitable Gambling?

Over the years I have been inundated with requests for charitable contributions. The more I donated the number of requests grew. The charities must share mailing lists. I am not complaining. I read all of the incoming mail to determine truly worthwhile causes. I have a soft spot in my heart for:

1. Wild horses, Mustangs, older horses, burros and donkeys.
2. Dogs, cats, pigs, chickens, sheep and any abused animal.
3. Wounded veterans, policemen and firefighters.
4. Indian causes especially Native Americans on remote reservations.
5. Religious groups of all kinds, especially older priests, nuns, monks, missionaries, preachers, et al.
6. Poor and sick people.
7. Specific diseases and ailments especially any little-known sicknesses not in the limelight.
8. Educational institutions.

Since innocent animals need help, I tend to want to help them first. I hope that I do not seem hard hearted but it may seem odd to favor animals over people sometimes but that is my nature; it just depends on the circumstances.

I am seriously worried about saving elephants, gorillas, chimpanzees and most endangered species whose habitat is shrinking based on human encroachment.

Over the years the nature of charitable requests has evolved from:

1. Simple requests without postage and many with prepaid postage.

2. Requests with free gifts including greeting cards – get well, thank you, Christmas and a variety of other items from ballpoint pens, playing cards, memo pads, toothbrushes, socks, bibs, etc.
3. Requests with money or checks enclosed to include one and two-dollar bills with warnings not to steal them. Nearly all charities want their one and two-dollar bills returned. Many requests include change glued inside the letter, some to assist with return postage. Checks included are to be returned or cashed. I'll return the check with my contribution or tear it up so that it cannot be cashed.

Some charities request reasonable contributions, but a few have listed presumptuous donation amounts, some often in the hundreds or even thousands of dollars. Many charities want monthly money payments from my bank account or charging my credit cards. Eventually a few charities want me to leave them money in my will or estate. Other charities include several envelopes, one for each month in the future. I dislike several envelopes. I prefer a one-time donation.

My sister Margie told me that she considers the deluge of requests as junk mail and she ditches many of them. When it comes to saving time sometimes, I admire her cold heart since she is busy with grandchildren who have an appetite for cash.

Some generous donors contribute large sums of money where they match other lesser donors with a similar amount. Many charities stated that contributions are multiplied two, three and many more times. Most charities seem to compete for the largest multipliers as a badge of honor or pride, perhaps rightfully so.

Within the last year the latest charitable rage is a sweepstakes or lottery type donations with potential prizes of from several thousand dollars to one million dollars. One donation will not win the money outright. There are usually three phases. If you do not enter each phase you forfeit the chance at the cash prizes and the charity garners these contributions. While it is said that no contribution is required to win, if you don't contribute some require that your entry for the prize be submitted on a three by five card by separate mail. I am not holding my breath to win any money, but I would donate most, if not all of it back to the charity and take a tax deduction, but I would not tell them that for obvious reasons.

Are all of these sweepstakes a form of charitable gambling? It is possible that charities have found out that sweepstakes generate the largest cash returns? As a Catholic I can remember listening to a sermon one Sunday on the evils of gambling. At the end of the sermon the priest reminded us about bingo which occurred every Wednesday night.

Epilepsy

My late brother John had epilepsy. John didn't always have epilepsy. Prior to the age of about 10 John was perfectly normal. We went nearly everywhere together. We lived in Harrison, New Jersey next to the RCA building. RCA had two city blocks of buildings and I think we lived next to an administrative headquarters. There was a bar down the block and one on the corner across the street. I shined shoes in the bars and my brother would sing occasionally. We kept the patrons entertained and made quite a bit of money for our age. We were rarely broke.

Railroad trains passed one block from our house and we felt the railroad car rumblings at all hours of the night. After a while we became used to the railcar sounds and they did not bother us. My brother and I walked to the railway yard and climbed all over the stationary train cars. When a flatcar was full of sand we would run along the roof of an adjacent boxcar and leap into the sand at full speed hurtling from the boxcar roof. I went into a caboose once to look around. I loved the interior of the caboose. It had a few leather-type beds and all the comforts of home. I yearned to be a railroad man; a fleeting desire on my part.

My brother and I loved to fish. We would walk to Kearny Park in Kearny, New Jersey to fish and ogle at the giant Goldfish in a cement fish pond for visitors to see. The Goldfish were actually giant orange Carp as I later learned. One day at Kearny Park, John and I were walking next to a baseball field where a softball game was in progress.

There were shouts of "Look out" when a softball struck John square on the head. John was knocked off his feet, flat on the ground. John shook off the effects of the blow while the ballplayers inquired if John had been hurt. John seemed to recover after a while, and we went on our way. I did not think about that event for decades, but I started to wrack my brain as to the cause of my brother's strange malady. I believe that my brother's epilepsy was attributed to that blow on the head.

Epilepsy is a strange ailment. I may be wrong, but I don't think it is a disease as we know it. My guess is that it is a brain disorder possibly attributable to a blow or birth where normal brain functions go haywire, short circuit or some more technical explanation would be far superior to my uninformed speculation.

My brother John lead a normal life until he had a seizure or epileptic episode (fit). When a seizure occurred, he would tense up, contort his face to a degree and fall occasionally. There was nothing that could be done except to keep John from hurting himself by striking an object during the seizure. I cannot describe the feelings of helplessness that I had when John had an attack. I am ashamed to admit, out of self-pride, I suppose, I was embarrassed in the midst of strangers since my brother was vulnerable and all I could do was watch helplessly. I wanted to help, and I couldn't. The ailment had to run its course. It could be over in a matter of minutes and things would return to normal.

John took pills for epilepsy. While the pills may have helped it did not cure him. In my reading on the subject I understand that there is a serious condition called a grand mal seizure, French for big malady. There may be something called a petite mal or a small ailment. Many famous people have had epilepsy and if I am not mistaken Napoleon Bonaparte had it. It is no comfort knowing that other people have the same problem.

John spent several years in the Air Force since he was perfectly happy and healthy otherwise. Perhaps his epilepsy was in remission because he was happy in the Air Force. Later in life John's heart gave him problems and he passed away.

I wanted to unburden my thoughts about what little I know about epilepsy that is based on my own experience with it. There must be a lot of unknowns about the function (or wiring) of the human brain. I must confess ignorance about causes and cures for epilepsy. Perhaps this essay may strike a chord or help someone else come to grips with and to cope with epilepsy; a road that was difficult to travel.

Hooray for Radio

When I was young, I never even heard of television; that makes me a senior citizen since I remember when. In my teens, televisions were expensive for a blue-collar family. My friend and I went to a neighbor's house to watch television on Tuesday night to watch Mr. Television, Milton Berle. That was the highlight of the week. Milton Berle was sponsored by Texaco and he was a joy to watch because he was so funny with his skits, mannerisms including impersonating women, a pure tour de force of talent. I had listened to a lot of comedy on the radio but Milton Berle's live comedic performances never lacked in its freshness and quality. Watching Uncle Miltie made me feel happy all over.

I grew up listening to radio programs. The programs included:

1. The Lone Ranger
2. The Green Hornet
3. Captain Marvel
4. The FBI in Peace and War
5. Tom Mix – A Western
6. The 64 Dollar Question
7. The Top Ten Tunes
8. The Shadow
9. Fibber McGee and Molly
10. The Life of Riley
11. The New York Giants
12. The New York Yankees with the great Mel Allen
13. Friday Night Fights - boxing
14. Superman
15. Amos 'n' Andy

16. The Bob Hope Show
17. The Fred Allen Show
18. News and weather
19. Quiz shows
20. It Pays to Be Ignorant – a comedy

There were a wide variety of detective, mystery, comedy, and westerns complete with sound effects to keep any listener with a vivid imagination entertained and wanting more.

In an era of television, it is understandably difficult to comprehend how it could be possible to be satisfied by merely listening to a program without seeing the action and interplay between the actors with their movements and facial expressions.

Enough by way of introduction, when I go to bed at night, I am more than content to listen to talk shows, political discussions, personal opinions, local events, weather, news, old radio shows, sporting events, music and practically anything that holds my interest. Since my standards are low it does not take much to hold my interest. I have a few complaints about radio that I need to get off my chest for the record.

1. I seem to get foreign language shows clearly while only a few shows in English come in clearly, especially when I am interested.
2. Occasionally I tire of sports chatter. I like sports but there are so many experts speculating that if our football team wins this weekend and if the Jets lose and if the Buffalo Bills win our Ravens will qualify for a wild card spot in the playoffs. I am making the aforementioned up out of whole cloth as an example. How long can these conjectures continue? Sometimes indefinitely. On a positive note there is a Raven's football announcer who is delightful because whenever the Ravens score, he shouts, "and the hay is in the barn." I spent some time on a farm.
3. I am not thrilled by rehashing the top ten news events of last year. Most people know last year's news, why exhume the body?

4. At the end of the year, I am interested in learning who passed away during the year. I am surprised and saddened to learn that people that I enjoyed, loved and admired are no longer with us. It is if I had lost a close friend or a member of my family or a beloved pet, so sad.
5. On Sunday mornings it is difficult to locate anything other than religious programs, real estate, investment shows and how to have enough money for retirement. Real estate agents tout their properties on Sunday mornings. Investment advisors will advise you if you have ½ million dollars or more. Many of the preachers are wonderful but a few get carried away. I love to hear preachers pronounce God as Gaawddhh. Am I being sacrilegious or am I merely amused by a warped sense of humor?
6. Is there any regular news or is all news breaking news? On a quiet news period the newscasters repeat the same news all day long and day after day making new news old news. One station said, "When news breaks, we fix it." I liked that weather forecasts, especially snow forecasts, tend to predict the worst-case scenario. As a result, when there is no snow or one inch instead of the predicted six inches, I breathe a sigh of relief, along with others.

At times I feel extremely lucky to be retired. When I hear dire traffic reports in the morning, I feel sorry for those who have to travel to work. With accidents and traffic snarls it seems nearly impossible for commuters to get to work on time. These are the times that try a Type A person's soul.

Sponsors for radio shows range from insurance companies, real estate agents, dentists, electricians, automobile repair people, roofers and home care for the elderly. Home care for the elderly is big business today and it is very expensive without mentioning the cost per day. Therefore, greater price transparency would be beneficial. Some ads appear so often they become tiresome. If the radio program is good enough, I can tolerate all forms of advertising which helps to pay bills. I may be used to punishment by now.

Despite its faults I love radio. Hooray for radio, its hypnotic effects make me happy and allows me to doze off at night, every night.

The Mosque

In college I had switched from four years attending college in the evening and arrived as a Junior as a regular daytime student. I enjoyed attending days and developed new acquaintances and friends since I was a people person and not anti-social. One of my newfound acquaintances asked me if I was interested in being an usher at the Mosque. The pay was three dollars plus tips. The token amount of money did not bother me since I had an opportunity to see top notch cultural events free at least once a month.

The Mosque was a venue/theater that hosted ballet, philharmonic orchestras, cultural events and famous singers and entertainers. I made a perfect usher since I was tall, lean, not mean, friendly, intelligent and I knew how to handle a flashlight. The bus from Hillside, New Jersey, my home, let me off near the Mosque, if necessary but I had an inexpensive second-hand aging car. While I lost money as an usher it gave me the chance to witness cultural events which provided me with an opportunity to be exposed to and hopefully to develop an appreciation of classical cultural events which I needed as a hard-working blue-collar person in search of new experiences necessary to smooth out any of my rough edges. I desperately wanted an injection of culture that I could get as an usher watching sophisticated accomplished singers, dancers and musicians who appeared and performed at the Mosque.

I loved my job as an usher. I had a chance to see and hear the New York Philharmonic Orchestra with the great Leonard Bernstein conducting. The Philadelphia Orchestra was conducted by Eugene Ormandy. I liked Eugene Ormandy immediately when he walked into the nearly empty lobby and said, "What's going on here today, is it the Budapest String Quartet?" Mr. Ormandy was not tall, and I may have detected a slight limp in him, but his personality was priceless since he obviously enjoyed kidding even at his expense. As a conductor he seemed ten feet tall in command of the highly talented symphony orchestra personnel. He had an attitude that he would not brook anything but perfection from his musicians all of whom were at the pinnacle of their musical skills that is the best of the best.

One day I had the immense pleasure of seeing the great conductor Leopold Stokowski. Leopold Stokowski was tall and lean with a magnificent head of white hair. He was an imposing figure as a conductor. At one point something happened that I had never experienced before. When Leopold Stokowski lifted his baton, he held the undivided rapt attention of each of the musicians. As he began conducting the orchestra sprang to life with the most wonderful classical music that left me almost dumbfounded. I vowed at that moment that if I ever purchased any classical philharmonic music it would be with Leopold Stokowski as the conductor. Not only was Leopold Stokowski an imposing figure as a conductor but every piece or movement was magnificent and a joy to hear. Even to my unsophisticated musical ears that were used to Gene Autry, Roy Rogers and popular singer's. Quality cannot be denied in any profession, I wouldn't think of it. But to me I thought that Leopold Stokowski made his musicians approach perfection at least in my mind. I loved the entire performance.

I had mentioned the Leopold Stokowski was an impressive figure. In reality, at a distance he appeared quite handsome or good looking. As an aside, I had learned that he had married one of the most strikingly beautiful women in the world. I had seen her photograph prior to her marriage, and I can attest to her beauty. I can only assume that Leopold Stokowski knew how to conduct himself as well.

One day there was a Scottish culture performance complete with a large ensemble of dancers with kilts and a cadre of bagpipers. The bagpipe music loudly and proudly filled the theater while traditional Scottish dancers performed. I liked the performance. Say what you will about the stinginess or tightness of Scots I don't believe any of it. I made the most in tips that day that I ever made in my time as an usher. I don't want to offend anyone, but I made the least number of tips from one sophisticated and intelligent audience.

One performance featured Johnny Mathis who to my amazement was extremely athletic. When he first appeared, he ran and dove headfirst over an obstacle, perhaps four feet high. Johnny Mathis landed on his hands tucked his head under and rolled 360 degrees springing back up on his feet fresh as a daisy and he was unabashedly confident. I don't recall if his first song started with, "Chances are . . ." but to my way of thinking Johnny Mathis must have been a high jumper based on his athletic ability which surprised everyone.

Nearly all performances were sold out. One time I saw the great Ray Charles and company. I'll never forget that show. Ray Charles had the audience in the palms of his hands. When he sang, "Tell your momma, tell your paw, I'm going to send you back to Arkansas" the crowd went wild in appreciation. The only way that I could describe it was that it exuded a 'joie de vivre' which I think is a joy of life. The French language is not only beautiful it is precise. It is essential that I use the exact proper expression to describe the atmosphere at the Ray Charles concert. It was obvious that the audience loved Ray Charles and his joy of life was reflected in his music. The audience atmosphere was infectious, and I was caught up in the overall happiness of the event. When Ray Charles sang "Georgia" you could hear a pin drop. The performance of Ray Charles became better and better with each new song. What a great talent Ray Charles possessed especially since he was blind. I cannot remember enjoying a show/performance more than that of Ray Charles. It just made me and the audience happy from head to toe and I was saddened when it ended.

At the Mosque I witnessed many ballet performances from Swan Lake to modern interpretive ballet. I did not think that I would like ballet, but I was wrong. I loved ballet including the dancer's sweeping and often exaggerated movements with graceful lifts and catches. It was nothing short of amazing. To think that these performers danced on their toes it is almost miraculous. I loved the graceful sweeping hand and leg movements which made the performance a thing of beauty. Beauty in ballet endeavors to approach perfection since the dancer's hand movements are graceful, precise and not erratic in any way.

Looking for Love at 82

I do not claim to be a 'culture vulture' but an appreciation of ballet developed within me and I am relaxed and give credit where credit is due, and it is certainly due with ballet and its talented performers. As an aside I later learned that one of our budding engineers became part of the ballet troupe. My friend was tall and skinny with long legs. My friend was fitted with tights, appropriate apparel and a spear. His job was to stand in the back of the set holding the spear as a guard. Our spear holder received the same applause as the prima ballerina and no doubt the audience was mesmerized by his mere presence, calm demeanor and passivity.

One performance featured Jose Greco, the world-renowned flamenco dancer who appeared with a large troupe of Spanish dancers. Mr. Greco was very serious about the presentation of his dancing and dancers. During the intermission I was backstage and similar to a fly on the wall I overheard Jose's earnestly discussing his final number which he called a production number. The final number featured the entire cast onstage shouting in Spanish, clicking their castanets and spiritfully stamping and lifting their feet to the music. The entire production number was the highlight of the show and Jose wanted the audience to enjoy the beauty and majesty of the spectacle, which I did. I had to admire Jose Greco's love of his art, his care and honest concern at pleasing the audience and the businesslike manner that he approached his task and responsibility in his attempt to achieve cultural excellence.

I don't recall many other performances other than the memorable pianist Arthur Rubinstein. Mr. Rubinstein exhibited a piano virtuosity without parallel. His hands seemed large and delicate so that he could easily reach the keys on the keyboard. He had an air of supreme confidence and he made the most complicated composition seem to be easy.

How could he possibly remember the lengthy complicated music? What an amazing talent? I may have seen a television show about Arthur Rubinstein, but his best critic was his loving musically intelligent wife. She made cogent remarks that improved his unimprovable performances. Her recommendations were very subtle. How she managed to detect ways to make his playing even better was a mystery to me but darn if she wasn't 100% correct when he incorporated her loving improvements, Mr. Rubinstein was lucky to have such a gifted wife.

I don't recall other concerts or performances at the Mosque. Perhaps concerts will emerge at some point from my subconscious, but it is too late for that now. Suffice it to say that I enjoyed being an usher. I liked the performances and the people that I ushered to their seats. If I could do it again I would, but that ship has sailed.

My Favorite Sandwich

As a youth my splintered family and I lived in the basement at my uncle's house on Long Avenue in Hillside, New Jersey. Next to my uncle's house was a small sandwich shop owned and operated by a man named Nick. Nick always wore a slightly discolored white apron over his nondescript shirt and trousers.

Directly opposite Nick's were several large buildings owned by the Bristol-Myers Corporation. Bristol-Myers manufactured a wide variety of health-related products. Bristol-Myers was a good neighbor hiring many people who made a good living there. Nick's sandwich business was primarily dependent on the appetites of the hungry Bristol-Myers employees.

I could smell the wonderful aromas emanating from Nick's place. Nick had one hot plate type grill. His establishment could not have been more austere. I do not recall any tables or chairs, but he may have had one or two chairs. I never used one since I was always on the go.

I don't know if you could call what Nick sold a sandwich as I know it. It was not a submarine, a hoagie, a grinder or whatever they are called throughout the USA. The bread was a ¾ inch thick frisbee-shaped with a hole the size of a half dollar in the center of it. The sandwich bread was cut in half, across the diameter whereupon the two halves were split in the center. Each half was cut to make a pocket in the bread that held the tasty ingredients. The ingredients were a small section of well-cooked Italian sausage with cooked slices of potatoes and green peppers. I do not recall any other ingredients.

I picked up a bread half stuffed with its delicious hot filling and began eating, that is wolfing it down. I was not exactly in heaven but close to it from a low budget pseudo epicurean point of view. One Italian sausage sandwich was enough besides being satisfying it was filling.

Years later, while in the Army, I returned on weekends and visited my fun-loving uncle on Long Avenue, and I would buy one enjoyable Italian sausage sandwich during each visit. Eventually Nick's place closed and was replaced by a photography shop owned by an uncle of one of my friends. Life is full of small disappointments, isn't it? It has been over five decades since I had my last Italian sausage sandwich. Since I don't eat pork anymore, by dietary choice, as a result I'll never eat another Italian sausage sandwich again. I suppose that if I was starving to death, I could be tempted to eat an Italian sausage sandwich in order to save my life. To quote Oscar Wilde, one of my favorite authors, "I can resist anything but temptation." In that event I may die with a smile on my face causing the mortician to be perplexed no end.

Modern Elections

Progressive determined that in the latest election they were 8,000 votes short. At that point a cadre of Progressives were turned loose scouring for votes. They looked for votes in attics, basements, hallways, closets, rest room stalls, under beds, in the library but not in the location designated for voting. Following the search, a host of likeminded sympathetic lawyers from many states descended to voluntarily interpret any questionable votes or to comingle them with legitimate votes of U.S. citizens. The Progressive lawyers analyzed and compared signature matches, punch hole chads to determine if the punch out was punched through completely. On some ballots with circles or ovals that needed to be filled in completely the Progressive lawyers determined if the circles and ovals were filled in enough to count as a vote. All the new votes unearthed were Progressive votes with no Republican votes. The Progressives wailed that every legitimate vote had not been counted and they inferred that voting racism was rampant, but they could not prove that claim in any way. The accusation was sufficient proof. When a Progressive won an election no claim of voter racism or shortfalls was heard since no doubt none existed when the preordained outcome occurred. Following a Progressive win civility was allowed to reign over the land once again; unlike their demeanor in a defeat often referred to as "sour" grapes.

Clutter

Clutter has been gaining on me as I slowly drifted into being a senior. As a youth I did not own anything beyond the bare essentials since money was in short supply. Unknown to me over the years items arrived but failed to depart expeditiously.

I now have an immense pile of receipts that are in boxes to act as proof in the event of a tax audit. It is surprising how many pieces of receipts, old checks and bills have accumulated even after I have shredded many more of these documents from time to time. Besides the old documents there are the books.

I have an aversion to throwing out old course books or joke books. I will probably not use my physics book, but it is a long disused friend of sorts and I hate to part with its company. During the last half century, I have consulted my old college physics book twice which barely justifies its continued presence.

I must have 25 or more joke books, many are quite voluminous. Every once in a blue moon I leaf through a joke book to refresh my memory and enjoy the jokes. The jokes are often not as funny the second time around, but then again similar to wine some of the jokes have improved with age. Some jokes that did not seem funny years ago are funny now as I have learned over the years and I say, "Oh, I get it now." I give my sister Margie many books that I have read, and she donates them to Goodwill. While I won't name them, some charities will not take used books.

Unfortunately, I dislike parting with any original writing or drafts of my five self-published books. It is strange that I have copies of the published books and I still retain the handwritten drafts and typed original pages of the text of each book. The day will come when I toss out everything except the published book, but not now.

On to the clothes. Since I retired, I have many clothes that I no longer wear on a regular basis. I'll wear a suit and tie to a wedding or a funeral, but these occur infrequently. Since my old acquaintances are dropping like flies, I attend more funerals than weddings, lately.

I still have many dress shirts and well over 100 neckties remaining. I had a fondness for neckties since I could express my questionable taste through my necktie. What can be more amusing than looking at someone with a tie too narrow, too wide, too long or too short? What were they thinking? A few ties appeared to be misguided or recycled Christmas gifts, selections by someone who needed new eye glasses or someone who could not distinguish between colors. No offense intended I am merely reporting a random observation, the exception rather than the general rule.

What to do with over 100 neckties? Out West we could have a necktie party (just joking). To date I have donated at least 50 to 100 neckties, but the remaining ones don't want to leave quietly. Old ties and old clothes are hard to let go. It is similar to losing an old friend. Did I mention that I had strange friends?

My wife's clothes are still attractive and many essentially new but now they have accumulated to the point that they are in several neat piles in a rarely used bedroom. The closets are jam packed, one blocked by piles of dresses. I don't believe that my wife has bought a new dress in many years, but she still has a great many fully functional, beautiful dresses. Luckily my wife is not a clothes horse. The day will come when my wife and I will have to bite the bullet and make our move to unclutter. I must have become lazy since procrastination agrees with me. It is the path of least resistance over the last few years and my resistance is low. Perhaps when we die my step-brother Frank will back up a dump truck and clean house, that is unclutter this place. When that happens all of my earthly clutter problems will be resolved once and for all.

Alex Gall

Mystery Telephone Call

Hello, is this the party to whom I am speaking? It is, good. Listen sweetheart, do you have a minute, we need to talk. Pick a subject, any subject. I don't get along with my nosey neighbors and since I am alone now, I need to talk to someone, or I'll burst. I like people usually. You are a person, I take it, and not a recording. How are things going or shouldn't I ask? Oh! It's a bad time for you today? What happened? He did what? Oh no! How could he? The beast. He left you flat. Why don't you get someone else to change your tire if it's flat? Do you have air? If I knew where you lived, I'd change it myself, but I don't want to run the risk of jeopardizing my disability payments. Call me when the dust settles, I'm in the book.

Mail Intimidations

There seems to be an inordinate amount of mail delivered to me lately. The mail consists mainly of bills, advertisements, charitable requests and junk mail. I am happy to receive mail that I can pitch out immediately since I have no interest or desire to read them. This includes the obvious junk mail. Most envelopes are designed to get my attention with visible small change, one- or two-dollar bills, free Forever stamps or free postage with three or more one cent stamps needed to pay towards the return postage.

The latest craze is a shift to prizes of money from several thousand dollars to a possible one million dollars. The sender allows me to choose the million-dollar cash payout in a lump sum, less taxes, or a payout over a 20- or 30-year period. I think that the advertisers would want me to take the grand prize over a 30-year period since the smaller amount is more affordable to them. However, at my age I won't be around 30 years from now to collect. If I can consequently, I choose the lump sum payment. Since the million-dollar prize requires the winner's number to match a 12-digit number I can't see how anyone can do that. It is more certain to be struck by lightning several times then to correctly match a 12-digit number. I'm sure a mathematician could be able to calculate the odds given enough time but even at that if he is not precise no one would blame him or live long enough to disprove him conclusively.

Enough chit chat, onward to mail intimidators, obvious and subtle. Lately envelopes received bear the following "intimidators":

Final Notice
Deadline
Urgent Renewal
Membership Renewal Due
Last Issue
Last Chance
Final Warning
Our records are incomplete
Urgent
SOS
Suspense

All of these intimidators are cumulative and in total more pressure than a normal person can bear. How drastic does the intimidation have to be to get my attention? Have the senders exhausted all intimidation possibilities? Can they threaten a voodoo curse in order to cloud my future?

If I live long enough, I would like to receive a letter that tells me that I have won a large sum of money with the check made out to me enclosed. All I get are letters saying that I am eligible to win the prize if I return the correctly completed final stage entry form plus a donation although the donation is not necessary and will not impair my chances of winning the grand prize or any of the lesser prizes. The last thing that I need is a new boat or a car in my driveway blocking the garage door. No doubt I would have to pay a tax on a car, or a boat and I would not want to part with the cash preferring it to draw the miniscule interest it could generate at today's shockingly low interest rates for anyone with some savings.

I have no trouble sleeping at night knowing that I don't expect to win a prize or be interrupted by a knock on my front door by a team of Publisher's Clearing House representatives with their photographer or television camera person.

With the return entry there are a few minor annoyances. The form contains a blank space for a sticker within or on the envelope. Sometimes the stickers necessary are cleverly hidden somewhere either in or on the envelope. In some instances, I have given up looking for the stickers and pitched the envelope and its contents in disgust. Several return envelopes have an area with a window to display the return address. Anyone in a drunken stupor may improperly insert the return address so that it is not visible, and the ball game is over.

Since I can't contribute to all charitable requests, I now have a backlog/pile of charitable requests stacked up nearly 15 inches high. The pile was much higher, but I made many donations and threw out the somewhat frivolous requests. If I hit a big prize payout, I will donate all or most of it to many deserving causes. I could use the tax deduction.

What is in the future regarding my avalanche of mail? I can't stop the bills. I can't stop anything for that matter. Pity the poor overworked mail person who has to deliver all of the junk mail house to house, apartment to apartment in all types of weather. I do not want to put anyone out of a job. I believe in capitalism, apple pie and the American flag. As a good citizen I'll just have to put up with the slings and arrows of the flood of daily mail. Help!

ACCOUNTANTS

Accountants are not always responsible, but they are often called to account.

Accountants don't trip but they are off balance from time to time.

There is no accounting for taste.

ACTING

I had to pull strings to work in a puppet show.

In Hollywood I had stars in my eyes, either that or someone punched me.

Joe was a budding actor. His first role was as a convict in prison; Joe considered it as a break out role.

ADAM AND EVE

Adam did not change his ways; he merely turned over a new leaf.

AIRPLANES

Never take a crash course in flying.

ALCOHOL

Pete finally quit his smoking habit; he began drinking.

Ralph's doctor told him to stop drinking but Ralph kept getting bombed until he was embalmed.

The union went on a wildcat strike as compared to a regular strike. In a wildcat strike the union members act wild because of the booze.

I was foaming at the mouth until I told the bartender to give me tap beer without the foam.

All persons were welcome at the tavern, bar none, with one exception, nuns were barred.

The boxer was punch drunk after he drank too much of the spiked punch.

I bought a nurse a drink and she nursed it.

In court, an alcoholic took the fifth, actually several fifths.

Pete tried to make homemade wine from grapes, but it didn't pan out because he botched up the batch.

AMBITION

There was no way that I could fill his shoes; his feet were too small.

Sam was a go getter. The problem was when Sam got it, he did not know what to do with it.

ANGER

Balloon experts don't get mad they just blow up.

Frustrated Pete said, "I've had it up to here." No one knew where here was.

When I started to boil, I was told to simmer down.

People in Silicon Valley don't get mad, but they have a chip on their shoulders.

ANIMALS

What type of fish is a standoffish?

Ralph said that he got a pig in a poke. Prior to that when Ralph was poked it was not by a pig.

Anteaters love to nose around in the wild.

A chicken is not criticized for laying an egg.

I bought my dog dark glasses and a quilted coat with a hood. Whenever I take her with me, she goes incognito.

I went on a wild goose chase. A wild goose is harder to catch than a domesticated goose; wild geese fly North.

Do foxes wolf down their food?

My wife feeds our cats Cornflakes, Raisin Bran, Garbanzo beans, ravioli, corn beef hash and all types of people food. The cats only eat cat food and my people food is gone.

The veterinarian handled the baby goat with kid gloves.

When pigs eat, they don't go hog wild; they pig out.

The ducks just didn't leave; they ducked out.

One day the early bird was late, and he got the bird.

Mouse: Take me to your liederkranz.

Alex Gall

I told everyone that 'A little bird told me.' To be honest, the little bird was actually a talkative parrot.

All at once Joe was mugged by a snail.

I found an alley cat in the street.

The racoon escaped because my hunting dog barked up the wrong tree.

In India, a king cobra was a basket case.

While a bird in the hand is worth two in the bush, a bird in the hand can get messy.

When was the last time anyone saw a bull in a China shop?

My cat was smart. She could operate a Xerox machine; she was a copycat.

Dorothy Parker's friend's cat died of curiosity.

I had a pet skunk, unfortunately the neighbors got wind of it.

The porpoise exclaimed, "It wasn't an accident; I did it on porpoise."

I had to put down my St. Bernard; she weighed too much.

Is a lazy, unemployed bull a bum steer?

Bees do not have a language; they use buzz words.

Kangaroos make progress by leaps and bounds.

I fed my cat the food that I took home in a doggy bag.

A duck was shot; police suspected fowl play.

I asked an elephant if she could keep a secret. She said, "I'm all ears."

My dog never did a day's work in her life; she said that she was on the gravy train.

At the pig picnic every pig went whole hog.

When Bob examined one dozen bugs, he explained, "These bugs are all bug-eyed."

Although my cat was curious, she died of old age.

What did the squirrel do with the dime that it found? Answer: He squirrelled it away.

ANXIETY

Jack jumped at everything. He jumped on the bandwagon, jumped the gun, jump started his car, jumped through hoops, jumped off the deep end and jumped to conclusions. All in all, Jack was jumpy and often referred to fondly as 'Jumpin Jack.'

APPEARANCE

Beautifully aged justifies age before beauty.

ARGUING

Why did the two porpoises argue? Answer: They were at cross porpoises.

Never argue in a hospital. That is no place to have bad blood between people.

I was told to bring it on, but no one told me what it was.

ARITHMETIC

In grammar school when I learned addition in arithmetic my teacher ended the lesson by saying, "Students, let me sum up what we have learned today."

ART

In art class the instructor asked Joe to paint a still life. Within one-month Joe went into the back woods and painted a still where bootleggers made white lightning.

AUTOMOBILES

No dear I'm not lost, I can read a map. Is that a road or a cow path?

There was a pileup on the highway. A truck driver with a semitrailer was delivering a load of new cars to a dealership.

The tow truck operator took my stalled car in tow.

Will the owner of the pink car with orange seat covers please stand up? I want to see what you look like.

Pete hitchhiked in a hearse. When he sat up three people fainted in adjacent cars.

I drove my car up a steep hill. I did not know if it could make the grade.

No one would go out to buy me cigars at the store, so I jumped in my car and ran over myself.

Phil had an automobile body repair shop. Business was brisk, and Phil was hard pressed to make a dent in the backlog.

A battery said to two jumper cables, "Don't get me started."

I got a great buy on a getaway car. The owner said he used it when he wanted to get away.

I wanted to take driving lessons until I learned that it was a crash course.

Sam made no progress because while his meter was running, he was parked.

Cars were bumper to bumper at rush hour.

People who repair cars that were in an accident do a bang-up job.

My tire dealer had a blowout sale.

For a laugh in the parking lot the attendants circled the wagons.

Car salesman to customer: "Sir, we don't sell used cars. What we sell is pre-owned, certified vehicles."

BANKING

I would not take out a bank loan at any rate.

My wife wanted me to open a savings account. To reassure her, I said, "You can bank on it."

Alex Gall

BARBERS

When my barber finished cutting my hair, he gave me the brush off.

My barber said, "I am not done until I do my part."

BASEBALL

Joe maintained that he did not strike out, he was just batting the breeze.

BEAUTY

Mary kept using so much vanishing cream that one day she vanished.

Thelma looked like a million dollars; she looked like something I had never seen.

A sales catalog featured a cosmetic storage tower for sale. I thought that if someone needed a tower to store cosmetics how long does it take to apply the cosmetics and how much help do they need?

Beauty advice: When applying lipstick do not apply any past your lips.

Try our new western round up bra, developed especially for aging cowgirls.

Stories that women tell in beauty parlors would curl your hair.

When I saw you, I got a lump in my throat. I didn't know if I was in love or if I was choking on the broccoli.

A witch was so ugly she refused to accept anything at face value.

The witches had a beauty contest. Right from the start things began to get ugly.

I couldn't call my girl beautiful. I called her looks interesting; similar to a Salvador Dali portrait.

BOXING

The boxer was not knocked out, he was just carried away.

Boxer's new year's resolution: "Don't take it on the chin."

Bad advice to a boxer: "Keep your chin up."

Bad advice to a boxer: "Knock yourself out."

Dorothy, my girlfriend, was a real knockout; she was an amateur boxer.

BRAINS

Mike was accused of having no brains, nothing upstairs. Mike dismissed the questions by saying "No matter."

Bill was accused of being stupid. Bill replied, "If you think I'm stupid you should see my grandfather, he is hunched over. I heard the sad story many years ago and repeated for posterity because if I don't someone else will."

Someone said to me, "We are of one mind." I replied, "When did you borrow my brains?"

BUSINESS

Instead of getting into the shrubbery business a broker started a hedge fund.

Tom failed as an apple polisher. Before he could polish the apple, he ate it.

Joe had a going out of business for the last time again sale.

Ralph was at a loss trying to determine exactly how his business had profited.

Jack's customers beat a path to his door because Jack had not mowed the lawn in front of his house for ten weeks.

A turf company ran a grass root's campaign.

The business had to close its doors because it left its windows open.

I went to a chain store and bought some chains.

CANDY

Are people who love lollipops on someone's sucker list?

Little Jimmy was a sucker for lollipops.

CANNIBALS

Two missionaries were sitting in a cannibal's cooking pot. One missionary said, "Brother James I think that we are in the soup now."

Cannibals don't gossip they merely chew the fat.

Visitors to the cannibal village were afraid of ending up being in the stew.

Cannibals prefer friars to soup chickens.

CARDS

Was it a stacked deck or was it that the cards were stacked against me? May I cut the deck?

CHARITY

When a zombie donated to a charity it was a dead giveaway.

Pete was always broke. The fault was that he was generous to a fault.

I was walking about in a big city that I was visiting when I encountered a person who asked me for a handout. I gave him five dollars and told him that under no circumstances should he spend it on food. I told him that he was overweight. Why compound the problem? I told him to buy a bottle of cheap wine, drink a glass, relax and think about looking for a job.

When did I become a member? I made a modest donation to a charity. I did not want to join anything and become a member. Now the charity wants me to renew my membership.

CHRISTMAS

It's Christmas; the more the merrier.

CLEANING

Joe said, "My used vacuum cleaner really sucks and am I happy?"

Sign in clothes cleaning shop: Two years on the same spot.

It is not possible to clean my wife's frying pan or other pots when she finished cooking. Soaking, scraping and Brilloing will not get the no stick frying pan clean. In the regular pots the oatmeal is firmly adhered to the bottom of the pot.

When the vacuum cleaner bag broke Mary bit the dust.

CLOTHES

Charles was a clothes designer. In his private life he cut quite a figure.

Jack said that he wore his heart on his sleeve, but it was summer, and Jack's shirts were all short sleeves.

COAL

Regardless of what they say about coal, there is no fuel like an old fuel.

COFFEE

In order to drink my container of coffee I had to flip my lid.

COMPLIMENT

I didn't know if it was a left handed or a back handed compliment but at least it wasn't underhanded.

CONDIMENTS

Black pepper is nothing to sneeze at.

COOKING

I barbequed on the roof of my apartment house. I was raising the steaks.

COWBOYS

Cowboys make decisions on the spur of the moment.

How often do rustlers take stock?

I was at the rodeo when I took the bull by the horns.

Rustlers take stock in America.

The cowboy was quick on the trigger but slow on the draw.

Bartender in Western saloon, "Partner did you just burp?" Customer, "No, I said that my name is Wyatt Earp."

CRIME

The mafia hitman was dressed-to-kill.

Mafia men don't eat a lot of beans. They are afraid that someone may spill the beans.

Tom was bent upon going straight.

Detective: "I'll tell you whodunit; Joe dunit. Now that that's settled, next case."

Policeman's inquiry: "Madam, show me exactly where the horse bit you."

The hit man took a Mafia taxi; he was being taken for a ride.

What do you take me for? Reply, "I don't know. How much do you have?"

CURSING

Bob was called every nasty name under the sun. When it became dark Bob was called a few more choice words.

DANCING

Miguel was either doing a flamenco dance or he just came in out of the snow.

When the music changed, we danced to a different tune.

The hula dancer insisted that her new home included a wiggle room.

A ballet dancer was not only alert, she was on her toes.

DATING

I told my girlfriend to get off of her high horse. What do you know, within one hour she returned on a smaller horse?

Jack's ding-a-ling girlfriend rang his bell.

A wrestler had a crush on his girlfriend.

I proposed to my girlfriend in my car. The car was parked in my garage with the garage door locked; I couldn't back out.

When I proposed my girlfriend did not bat an eyelash, she batted both eyelashes.

I said to my girlfriend, "What did you have in mind?" Lulu replied, "Nothing, my mind's a blank."

My girlfriend was full of wonder; in a word wonderful.

My girlfriend's legs were stocking stuffers.

My girlfriend said that she had qualms about me. I said, "What does a qualm look like?"

My girlfriend Lulu bragged, "I have you in the palm of my hand." I replied, "Don't be ridiculous, your hand is too small."

I hugged my girlfriend Lulu and said, "How does that grab you?"

John promised his girlfriend the moon. When they broke up, he mooned her.

I gave Brenda, my date, the once over lightly. Unfortunately, Brenda didn't take it lightly.

I was sweet on my girlfriend; I kept calling her sugar.

I wanted to settle up. My girlfriend wanted to settle down; things were unsettled.

I went out on a blind date. To my surprise the lovely young lady sold me window blinds.

My date Joan was an x-ray technician; it didn't take long for her to see through me.

Tom dated a telephone operator, but she had her hang-ups.

My girlfriend Ivy grew on me.

I called her my dear because she was expensive.

DEATH

Jack thought that he had breathed his last but as luck would have it that thought didn't last.

Joe was alive and kicking. Joe said, "I can't kick when I am dead."

Sam forgot the key to death's door and was told to come back a lot later.

Grave diggers are used to digging up the dirt.

Tom was gone and forgotten but his brother was not forgotten because he owed money.

People were dropping like flies. Business was so brisk that they added a graveyard shift at the cemetery.

The cemetery owner was accused of harboring grave thoughts.

The mortician bragged that he had a layaway plan.

DEBATING

I did not agree to disagree; I agreed to be agreeable.

DELIVERIES

Federal Express merged with UPS. The new company was called Fed-Up.

DENTISTS

Question to dentist: Do you solemnly swear to pull the tooth, the whole tooth and nothing but the tooth? Answer: I does.

DOCTORS

The doctor took his own medicine; it was a bitter pill to swallow.

I took my cardiologist's advice to heart.

I complained to my optometrist that my eyes were on the blink.

Sam was itching to see his dermatologist.

My doctor was a specialist. He specialized in walletectomies.

An allergist did something rash.

DRACULA

Dracula and his brother rarely argued but when they did, they were at each other's throat.

Count Dracula didn't die he just came to a dead end.

DREAMS

Rick built castles in the air; his wife Thelma furnished them.

ECONOMICS

The person who founded Trickle Down Economics was trickled on.

EDUCATION

I knew the questions to the test inside and out, but I did not know the answers.

My teacher did not call us names; she called us by our names.

In study hall Joe was a quick study.

Paul was too slow to pull a fast one.

Sam could not make heads or tails of a nickel; he was buffaloed.

I was absent from school so often my teacher said, "Alex, absence does not make the heart grow fonder."

I was absent minded. Whenever I was absent no one minded.

I waited quite a while to take a course on watch repair. I waited so long I exclaimed, "It's about time."

Pete wasn't the best of the best; he was the best of the worst or the worst of the best.

After I counted to 144, I grossed out.

Was it a stroke of genius or did the genius have a stroke?

In the Boy Scouts I learned the ropes, but my scoutmaster told me that I was too young to tie the knot.

My back was against a wall when I noticed a sign that said, "Don't back up."

Pete was black and blue, luckily, they were his high school colors.

In first grade my math teacher had my undivided attention.

Newscaster: I know that we don't know what we don't know.

EFFICIENCY

Charlie saw some slack on the ground, and he picked it up.

EGGS

Humpty Dumpty was not a bad egg, but he finally cracked.

ELECTRICITY

Sam was kept in the dark until he paid his electric bill.

Millie was young and beautiful. She didn't mind people crying on her shoulder, but she said, "I'm running out of shoulders."

ENGLISH

I gave my word, but I decided to break it. I made the word noon into two words, no and on.

The Morse code operator decided to dash off a message.

ENTERTAINMENT

Tom's company built barges. Whenever Tom went to a party, he just barged in.

Mr. Ferris was a big wheel at the carnival.

ENVIRONMENT

Lately the EPA is grasping at straws; that is plastic straws to be precise.

EVOLUTION

The theory that men descended from apes drives me bananas.

EXERCISE

I was out of breath when someone told me to save my breath.

The convict did a stretch in an elastic band company.

FAIRY TALES

At long last, Rapunzel finally let her hair down.

FAMILY

Mother's advice to daughter: Do not leave any messages on the bathroom mirror with your lipstick. I have to clean that mess off. Have you ever tried to get lipstick off of a mirror?

Jane had kissing cousins but avoided kissing them incessantly.

Cannibals: Mom always liked you best. Reply: That was because mom had good taste.

When Sam was born the doctor said to his mother, "I have bad news, your son pulled through."

John found out that he didn't have a family tree; he had a family shrub.

My mother-in-law was a back-seat driver until I bought a motorcycle.

What a strange family. Everything that Tom said to his brother went into one head and out the other.

Jack took after his father. Jack's brother, Romeo, took after women.

Lulu was with child. It wasn't her child, but her neighbor's child.

My brother was an only child.

The teenage drivers were acting like a bunch of cowboys; they circled their wagons.

FARMING

Mary the farm wife was hand milking her cow, Buttercup. Some of the milk that did not hit the target was beyond the pail.

Many farmers don't give it a second thought they just plow into their work.

FASHION

Expensive hats never went to my head.

The Scotchmen's clothes were out of kilter.

The dress designer exclaimed, "I don't want anyone to cramp my style."

Della was dressed to the nines. When she was dressed to the tens she was overdressed.

My wife said that I would never change; that is when I decided to buy a new wardrobe.

News flash: Minnie Pearl bought a hat with no strings attached.

Mary was window dressing until the owner of the store told Mary to dress somewhere else.

FISHING

I wanted to get a line on fishing.

Tom was hooked on fishing, hook, line and sinker.

FLOWERS

I went into a florist shop and came out smelling like a rose. What did I step in?

FOOD

Tim couldn't cut the mustard. At that point Tim decided to use catsup.

Tom loved couch potatoes. He said that besides potatoes he had couch radishes, cucumbers and a handful of onions.

Overweight Tom was a roll model at the bakery.

Alex Gall

The sales catalog featured a square titanium frying pan. Since I haven't had a square meal in a long time, I may just buy a square frying pan.

The loose nuts were housed in a large box often referred to as a nut case.

My hotdog had a high turnover rate on the grill.

Our takeout food was delivered.

I bought some Bubba soda; it went with my Bubba gum.

Lunch wouldn't be lunch if it wasn't souped up.

Ralph developed a green thumb; he was coloring Easter eggs.

In order to remove all of the meat you have to cut to the bone.

In Maryland when seasoning crabs don't keep the Old Bay at bay.

One night for supper I was hungry for Chef Boyardee Ravioli. I asked my wife to heat up Ramen Chili Soup followed by ravioli. What I got was chili soup with ravioli in the soup. It was poor chili soup and soupy chili that did not go well with grated parmesan cheese.

To tenderize meat, buy meat tenderizer and rub it in.

The aging chef's hair was salt and pepper.

Eating too many cherries soon become the pitts.

After the potato chip bag broke the chips were down.

Luckily my walnut was between a rock and a hard place.

I could not bring home the bacon; my wife was a vegetarian.

Chefs don't compliment each other, they butter up each other.

I was hungry. I did not know whether to say gee whiz or Cheese Whiz.

Some guy from Vermont tapped my telephone. He obtained enough syrup from it to completely cover one pancake.

I went to some trouble preparing your breakfast; take the trouble to eat it.

It was announced on the news that Romaine lettuce was contaminated with e-coli causing severe illness. All Romaine lettuce had to be thrown out including Romanian Romaine.

Stranger, are you hungry? You are. How do you like your beans? Reply: Cooked.

Sign in a German butcher shop, 'Our sausages are the wurst.'

FRANKENSTEIN

Frankenstein said, "Will I ever meet my maker?"

FRIENDS

In a movie Sophia Loren met Raquel Welch and they became fast friends; actually, they became bosom friends.

Two ladies had a gentlemen's agreement.

I saw an ad for a companion table in a sales catalog. I suppose that if you are short of companions you could talk to the table.

Like father, like son but I did not like either the father or the son.

Jack was a low down, dirty, no good, lying, unreliable, cranky, ornery, mean, deceitful bum and those were his good points.

Was Joe friendly or not? At the entrance to his house Joe had an unwelcome mat.

John went to a masquerade party as a giant elastic band; all went well until he snapped.

Pete said that he wanted to have a word with me. I wandered what the word was.

Jack said, "I hope that you have a thick skin. I said, "What do I look like a navel orange?"

Jack was out of sight but not out of mind; then again, he may have been out of his mind.

Tom was a good egg; he always kept his sunny side up.

Lulu rocked the boat; luckily it was a large boat.

I backed up into a party when I was told not to butt in.

In high school I sat next to a girl named Jill Perfect. I was as close to perfect that I would ever get.

FURNITURE

My chair was very old; in reality it was on its last legs.

GAMBLING

I won the poker game because I played my cards right.

I aced the poker test.

Dracula played poker with a skeleton. When the skeleton lost it made no bones about it.

A classic gambler's comment at the Thoroughbred race track, "I'd like to break even, I need the money."

I didn't know why I was at a loss, maybe I should quit gambling.

A bookmaker and his client were at odds.

At a Thoroughbred race track it takes no brains to back the wrong horse.

I needed an even break so that I could break even.

GAMES

The name of the game is parcheesi, is that spelled correctly?

GARDENING

I had a stake in my tomato plant.

I bought some topsoil, but it wasn't dirt cheap.

GHOST

In order to write his life story Casper hired a ghostwriter.

GOLD

My pay dirt was played out when there was no flash in the pan.

GOLF

Mary said to Tom her date, "Do you want to play around?" Tom's reply, "I haven't touched a golf club in years."

Pete went golfing as a matter of course.

HAIR

Should someone with a bald head put a cap on it?

HALLOWEEN

At Halloween I hired a skeletal crew.

HANDWRITING

I wanted to make my mark. I was told just sign with an X.

HAPPINESS

Sam was feeling his oats. When he finished with his oats, he felt some wheat.

HEALTH

I bought a magnetic back support; it attracted paper clips.

Melvin had a knee jerk reaction when the doctor hit him in the knee with a small hammer.

I'll admit that I was in the hot seat; I was in the sauna, wasn't I?

The lovely lady chiropractor turned my head.

I needed a shot in the arm. Unfortunately, my doctor obliged.

Mary fired her massage therapist but told him to keep in touch.

I couldn't afford the visiting nurse, so I married her. Now she visits other people during the day.

When I left the stuffy room and went outside it was like a breath of fresh air.

My wife put a band-aid on my cut finger, kissed it and said that it was all better. I said it would be better if it wasn't cut.

Tom was walking around barefoot. He complained that someone had knocked the socks off of him.

Since I sleep late the crack of dawn for me is noon.

A masseuse rubbed me the wrong way.

I did not want to go for a long walk, but I took it in stride, eventually.

What do you do when you have a few loose screws? Answer: Tighten the screws.

Both of my hands were close at hand.

Pete had a screw loose which he remedied after he bought a screwdriver.

For a moment I lost my head, now everyone is out looking for it.

I went out on a blind date. Everything was going great until her seeing eye dog bit me.

If you have your health, you have everything. If you don't have your health, you have something.

My role model: Anyone who lives to be in his nineties and maintains that he never exercised a day in his life.

HEIGHT

Tim loved the short end of the stick. He always came up short; his nickname was Shortstuff.

Joe returned from a visit to Ireland where he said that he had kissed the baloney stone. I remarked, "That's Blarney."

HISTORY

In court the mummies could not beat the wrap.

Mummies are wrapped up in themselves.

HUMOR

Paul did not know if he was at his wit's end or if it was the end of his wit.

Max had the last laugh because it took him a lot longer to get the joke.

Question: Do you solemnly swear? Yes, I solemnly swear, is that it? Sometimes I swear while laughing does that count?

Don't stop me if you've heard this one.

IDENTITY

Jack said that it was neither fish, flesh, nor fowl. As a college graduate Paul said that it was a rock.

INSULTS

Was I told 'carry on' or did someone just call me an ugly bird?

I was impressed by the fact that whenever you spoke you had difficulty getting your foot out of your mouth.

I am perfectly normal, similar to you, that is if you were ever normal.

INSURANCE

Don got hit in the head with a baseball. His insurance company paid him a lump sum settlement.

INVENTIONS

John invented an unboggling machine to help people who have had their minds boggled. You just never know.

JUSTICE

The judge's plumbing was out of order.

I had my day in court; at night court.

LAUNDRY

During laundry day my wife said, "I finally had to throw in the towel, it 'was dirty.'"

LAWYERS

All lawyers are great and nice people, deep down.

During my time as a jurist I was seated for days on end.

A lawyer kept his own counsel.

LAZINESS

You don't have to be goofy to goof off.

LIES

John made his bed and he would lie in it because he had trouble being honest.

LIFE

Jack's life flashed before his eyes and was it boring.

I wanted to turn the tide, but the tide wasn't ready.

It was early in the morning when we saw the light of day.

In order to cushion the blow, I bought a cushion.

Mike wanted to wear out and not to rust out.

LIGHT BULBS

I don't like to make light of light bulb jokes.

LIVING

When my troubles went down the drain; I called the plumber.

LOVE

My girlfriend said that it was all over. I said, "Well, all right, I'm all shook up and all systems are go, go, go."

I don't like to brag about my love life, but I was told that the Statue of Liberty was carrying the torch for me.

Kiss me you fool. Reply: I'd be a fool not to kiss you.

I was either crazy in love or I was losing my mind.

Son: "Mom, I think that I am in love." Mom: "Son, you must be because you have a silly, sloppy look on your face."

John: "Marsha, your eyes are the windows to your soul, unfortunately the shades are down."

At the party Joe was running out of ice for mixed drinks when he told his girlfriend, Lulu, "I only have ice for you."

Marsha: "John, I think that I am in love; I'm burning with desire." John: "Marsha, your forehead is hot, you may be running a fever. You may not be burning with love, just burning."

John: "Marsha, what can I do to convince you to love me?" Marsha: "How much money do you have? If you were worth millions, I could fall in love quicker."

The college student said, "Make love, not war." The Army general said, "I love war."

Mary and Bob were dating. Both had been saving up their love. When asked they both maintained that there was no love lost between them.

Now that I have broken up with Darlene how can I get her tattoo off my chest?

Dating a French lady: Your lips tell me No! No! but there's oui oui (pronounced we we) in your eyes.

My feet were on the ground, but my head was in the clouds; was I in love?

When I tripped, I told my girlfriend that I was falling for her.

Sam's girlfriend told him to go jump in a lake. Sam replied, "Did you have any particular lake in mind?"

Jane fell in love with an alien. Jane said that he was out of this world.

My girlfriend Sheila made my head spin until I told her to stop hitting me in the head with her umbrella.

Tom was a narcissist; he went to Lover's Lane by himself.

John sang at the top of his lungs from the bottom of his heart and with a quiver in his liver.

My girlfriend Jane was a breathtaking until I realized that she was choking me.

He left you flat. Why don't you get someone else to change your tire if it was flat?

LUCK

John said that he had a fickle finger, but his other fingers were less fickle.

Tom had no luck as luck would have it.

MAGIC

Magician: "Ladies and gentlemen, keep an eye on this trick. My fingers will never leave my hands."

When the magician used every trick in the book he decided to disappear.

MAIL

Stamp out mail, or is it mail without a stamp?

MANAGEMENT

Bill weighted 300 pounds. Bill was supervisor and said that he was large and in charge.

My boss was a large cog in a small wheel.

Jack was a small fish in a big pond.

I was in front; how could I bring up the rear?

MANNERS

Don bit the hand that fed him, but he promised that the next time he would use a knife and a fork.

MARRIAGE

John was not the apple of his wife's eye. She said that John was more like a thorn in her side.

My wife and I made ends meet by sitting back to back.

My wife was my jogging partner; I called her my running mate.

During the divorce process Mary referred to her husband as her insignificant other.

Mary married so often she had a wash and wear wedding dress.

Suitor: "Mr. Jones, I'd like to ask for your daughter's hand." Mr. Jones: "What's wrong with the rest of her?"

Sally did not marry the best man, she married the groom.

The danger of marrying a cousin is that in church you could have all of the relatives on the same side of the aisle.

I bought my wife a jewelry box. I suppose the next thing she'll want is jewelry.

I stopped in my tracks because my wife said that I was tracking mud all over.

Joan liked to keep house. Whenever Joan was divorced, she kept the house.

The cowboy said that when he was married, he was roped into it.

I was a runner. My wife and I ran around together for one year before we married.

I'll stand in for anyone but the groom.

My wife was taking a bubble bath for nearly one-half of an hour. I was frustrated so I finally pulled the plug on her.

Joe denied that he was henpecked, and he was about to express an opinion, but then his wife said that he did not have an opinion.

Tom's marriage was a classic case of give and take. Tom gave and his wife took.

Make your choice, either stay or go. Reply: "I'm going to stay."

How long have you been married? Answer: Too long.

I put my wife on a pedestal; I married a statue.

MATHEMATICS

Max was a mathematician, but he could not put two and two together.

A calculator is something that you can count on.

MEDICINE

Researchers of our pills received a Nobel prize nomination but not for our pills.

MERCY

The quality of mercy is not strained, it is filtered.

MILITARY

The drill sergeant said, "About face!" I replied, "What about my face?".

In the Army I was not AWOL, I was just off base.

Do Navy people take liberties?

Sam stood out in the Army because all the soldiers in his line took one step backwards.

When Joe was drafted into the Army, he wanted to pull rank but there was no one lower.

John said that he would jump at the chance to be a paratrooper.

Jack returned his parachute. He said it didn't work and "Do you have an aspirin? I have a headache."

Paul wanted to be a sniper in the Army; he gave it his best shot.

MODESTY

At first blush was hard to determine because she blushed so often.

MONEY

My checkbook was off balance.

I was in debt. I maintained that if I was taller, I wouldn't be in over my head.

The best way to stretch a buck is to make money out of rubber.

If I had been taller, I would not have been caught short.

Ralph said that he finally had a nest egg. He said that he took it from a chicken with a long memory.

None of the aristocrats welcomed Tom into their social circle because he was considered new money an interloper and a social climber. In his defense Tom exclaimed, "Just because I embezzled the money doesn't make me a bad person. I suppose that none of you ever stole anything. I should fit right in."

When Tom's car stopped on a dime he backed up, got out and picked it up.

In Ireland, in some places your money may be Dublin.

I wanted to foot the bill, but the waiter wanted me to take my foot off the bill.

I wrote a check in the rain; it was a raincheck.

Where do pigs keep their money? Answer: In mutual funds and not in a piggy bank.

It turned out that the bottom line was the last line on the page as usual.

At all costs spare no expense.

Mary couldn't get a rise out of her dough, so she put it in the bank.

Silver is a great investment; it's running out. It used to be running in, but it got tired.

John was accused of being filthy rich. In his defense John exclaimed, "That is not true, I shower regularly."

MOOD

I was at a low ebb. What could I do the tide went out?

My girlfriend said that I lost my mojo. Since I have never seen a mojo, I did not know what to look for or where.

MUMMIES

A mummy was a narcissist because he was all wrapped up in himself.

MUSIC

The band had a great drummer; he never seemed to miss a beat.

Tim liked music; he said that it struck a chord.

Sam was a windbag until he learned to play bagpipes.

As a trumpet player I wanted to horn in.

Being a bell ringer took its toll.

Two musical composers settled an argument by comparing notes.

NAMES

Paul was a namedropper until he went to Poland.

Bellboy to hotel guest: "Sir, are you somebody, are you famous?" Visitor's reply: "Am I famous, my name is John and if you will check you will soon discover that I have many rooms in this very hotel named after me."

Ben used to be straight, but now he is gay.

NEWS

Radio station: We cover all the breaking news from the outhouse to the state house to the White House.

On the news: Someone had a newfound hatred for President Trump. Question: What happened to the old hatred; wasn't it good enough?

When the news breaks, we fix it.

The bad news is that there is no good news.

NUDISTS

After the nudist 100-yard dash the winner exclaimed, "I'm on a winning streak."

John was very generous. While he lived in a nudist colony, he would give you the shirt off of his back.

OBSERVATIONS

I received a gourmet food catalog where the prices were so expensive that if I ordered anything from the catalog the catalog owners could spend one week at Monte Carlo gambling as well as enough to afford to send one student to a prestigious ivy league college for one week.

I never tire of reading books for entertainment. I wish that I could read many more of them. I can only experience a limited number of events during my lifetime. Reading provides a vicarious view of others whose lives are frequently much more interesting and appealing. If nothing else reading provides the means to know some of what I have missed.

Opportunities look bigger going than coming.

PAINTING

John had a brush with painting; maybe he should use a roller.

PEOPLE

In Holland most people go Dutch on dates.

PERSONALITY

Joe never raised a hand to a woman unless it was in self-defense.

So many people have come out of the closet. I wish that my closets were that large.

Your Honor, I may be a gay crook, but I promise to go straight.

I was in a state of mourning in the afternoon.

PHYSICIANS

Two cardiologists had a heart to heart talk.

Plastic surgeons get under your skin.

PLANTS

Did the founders of Burpees go to seed?

PLUMBERS

I called my plumber and told him that I had a problem with my commode. I asked him to come over and look into it.

My plumber fixed everything but the kitchen sink.

POLICE

Jim, the detective, said that the suspect was neither here nor there. He decided that the suspect was somewhere else.

The policeman asked Mary to pull over. Mary rolled down her car window and said, "It's not a pullover, it's a sweater."

Police reported that a heavy-set criminal was at large.

Jack was hit in the head with a small battery that had been thrown at him. The policeman charged the battery thrower with assault with a battery.

After the knife fight the police were looking for the smoking gun.

Officer, I was taken for a ride, I was not hitchhiking.

The police grilled the chef.

The police wanted to grill an oyster, but it clammed up.

Mary gave the detective the slip; after which she was arrested for indecent exposure.

A goat thief got my goat.

I was above the law. I rented a room above a police station.

POLITICS

A woman's movement representative exclaimed, "They put up a good fight, but we finally captured the House." Evidently the guards at the House of Representatives were overwhelmed by a sheer force of numbers. While the guards were captured, they were not abused, tortured, humiliated or taken prisoner. The guards received a severe tongue lashing by their captors, but they were not humiliated in front of the women despite intense giggling by the women when the house guard's backs were turned.

John tripped backwards and landed squarely on his tail sitting on the ground. In his defense John said that it was his fallback position.

Mayor's comment: "There is plenty of money in this city, it is just in the wrong hands. That is, if it is not in my hands, it's the wrong hands."

"I personally think." is what a guest said on a televised political talk show. Why not just say, "I think" isn't that personal enough?

The President said I want a wall, I don't want to go AWOL.

Read my lips, do you read me?

Are Progressive policies nothing but a free-for-all?

When the candidate that I had voted for won the election I was politically correct.

Stand up and be counted; sit down and be overlooked.

I wanted to vote a straight ticket but what could I do the ticket was bent.

President Trump was acting like a dictator; he said, "Mrs. Jones take a letter."

POOL

In the poolhall Jack was used to going from rack to ruin.

PROBLEMS

I was in square two and I could not go forward; what could I do? I went back to square one.

PSYCHICS

When I visited a psychic, I became psyched out.

My psychic was behind the times; she read last week's tea leaves.

Before making any predictions, a psychic had to be psyched up.

PSYCHOLOGISTS

The psychologist walked down the street dragging a couch on wheels. He said that he was making a house call.

READING

I bought a magazine table through a mail order catalog. Now I have to buy subscriptions to any number of magazines to place on my magazine table. I may even read some of the magazines or donate some really old magazines in my basement to my dentist.

RELIGION

If I go to heaven, there won't be anyone there that I know.

Speaking to God: Hello, hello, Am I speaking to God? Oh! You are not God. Ok. I've been holding on the telephone for over 30 minutes listening to elevator music then I heard your heavenly voice. I said, "God, is it you; I've waited for an eternity?"

The preacher had a holier-than-thou attitude.

People in hell don't get mad, but they do get burned up.

John did not have bats in his belfry until he purchased a church.

When Sam arrived in hell, he received a warm welcome.

Is it a sin to kiss a nun? Answer: No, unless you do it religiously.

Paul started a new religion; he wanted to lord it over everyone.

My religious psychologist prayed on my nerves.

I wanted to turn the other cheek, but I had been slapped twice. What to do?

Lott's wife was the salt of the earth.

The priest and the minister were not arguing, but they were at cross purposes.

On his plane flight the Pope looked out the window and blessed the earth; it was a blessing in the skies.

The man who rang the church bells died; now he is a dead ringer.

The devil was up to no good.

REVENGE

Jim had it coming. He also had it going.

ROLE MODELS

A giant is someone you can look up to.

RUMORS

Sam said that he heard it through the grapevine. What do you know a talking grapevine?

We wanted to get the inside dope that is why we came to see you.

RUNNING

The convict maintained that he was not in the marathon but admitted that he was on the run.

During my daily jogs I ran past a mill. I was known as the run of the mill runner.

SAFETY

Don't be in a cave during a cave in.

SALES

I was bored; the variety store lacked sufficient variety.

Sam said that it was no go, no sale, no kidding, no deal and no dice. Do I make myself clear? Reply, "Yes."

You have to take steps to sell shoes.

Sign up for our real estate course. Seating is extremely limited. Once the stadium is full it is standing room only.

Seating is limited. Once the stadium is filled no one will be allowed to enter.

SEAFOOD

The world was my oyster until my doctor told me that I was allergic to shellfish.

SENIORS

I was not old, I was just getting along in years.

How old do I have to be to have a senior moment?

SHOES

The sales catalog featured an over-the-door shoe rack in order to see your shoes at a glance and smell any that are not kissing sweet.

SHOOTING

Were they poor shots, I'll say? The safest place to be was in the line of fire.

SHOPPING

Sally went window shopping. She purchased four windows. Her husband said, "Your window shopping is becoming a pane."

SIGNATURE

I am sure that it isn't John's signature. Perhaps it is merely a slip of the pen.

SILENCE

If you are going to hold your tongue wash your hands first.

SINGING

Dracula's wife's singing could wake up the dead.

You mean that someone sings worse than I do? I find that hard to believe. I became a vegetarian by gathering the fruits and vegetables thrown at me while singing.

SLEEP

Pete bought a circular bed; he is now accused of sleeping around.

Trying to sleep on ice must be spine chilling.

Who would want to sleep on a bed of roses; that appears to be a thorny question?

Even Mrs. Dracula needs her beauty sleep.

Jack was in a boat when he drifted off to sleep.

On an overcast day I woke up bright and early.

SMOKING

When you smoke expensive cigars does your money go up in smoke?

Some smokers have pipe dreams.

SPACE

The astronaut wanted to be spaced out or was it in outer space?

SPEAKING

John said, "Can a ventriloquist put words into my mouth, I'm no dummy?"

SPEECH

That just shows to go you or is it goes to show you?

I'm here on behalf of the mayor. Response: "If the mayor be half who be the other half?"

Does anything self-explanatory go without saying?

Famous last words, "Let me out of here."

Some tongue twisters are easier done than said.

I went to a bowling alley to strike up a conversation.

John exclaimed, "I'm going to swear off cursing or I'm going to stop cursing, I swear."

Eating your words is hard to do but swallowing your words is tougher.

Ralph had the last word; it was "what?"

I purchased a pointer to point out salient points during my memorable speech. Without the pointer the speech was pointless.

Some people end a conversation with, "I'm going to let you go. . ." Response, "Thank God, you have been choking me too long."

I was told to be brief. Hearing that I felt confident because this morning and every morning I wore briefs, as usual.

SPIDERS

The spider appeared unconcerned that it was hanging by a thread.

SPORTS

The punter said, "I get a kick out of football."

The race started off with a bang.

After buying the helmet he threw in the football to boot.

My batting coach told me to keep my eye on the ball.

Tim, the marathon runner, said, "I'm in it for the long run."

Ralph had two strikes against him, but he was used to it; he was a baseball player.

Good advice to a novice swimmer: "Keep your head above water."

In order to get a level playing field we brought in a grader.

While Jack was at his best, he came up short on the basketball team.

Iggy, the boxer, was knocked out when his opponent beat him to the punch.

Everyone at the poolhall is behind the eight ball at one time or another.

In tennis, first come first served.

At my age in order to get the ball rolling I would have to learn how to go bowling.

Joe was at the pool until he went off of the deep end.

I went to bat for the baseball player.

The guy that gave me a massage was out of touch.

Good basketball players don't foul up on the foul line.

On a football team the punter does it for kicks.

At the track meet all the runners in the mile run wore battery warmed socks. They were told that it would be a heated race.

The football game was so boring that there were no highlights only low lights.

STATUES

The statue in the New York Harbor was always at liberty.

Marble statues begin as a chip off of the old block.

STRENGTH

John stopped arm wrestling once he got the upper hand.

SUCCESS

I was told that I was teetering on the brink of success. I teetered and teetered until I tottered.

TELEPHONE

Telephone call: You don't say! You don't say! You don't say! What did he say? I don't know he didn't say.

TELEVISION

I watched television shows too long. Instead of saying, "Let me explain" I say "Let me esplain, Lucy."

THINKING

Sam's brainstorm was more of a gentle breeze than a full-fledged brainstorm.

TIME

Every dog had his day, but every calendar has its days.

Is Big Ben in London big time?

It took a while to do the measuring. At length we measured the width.

While away Pete whiled away his time for a while.

To be on time I bought my watch just in time in a timely manner.

Was it quick? Answer: "It was quick as a bunny, faster than greased lightening, lickety split, in a flash, in an instant and in a New York minute but I'll respond in due time."

Question: How long is once in a while? Answer: A little longer than now and then.

At the end of the day it's night.

TRASH

Does trash go to waste?

TRAVEL

I wanted to take a vacation, but I was broke. I looked through travel brochures and found a vacation spot that I could afford. The vacation spot was named, 'The Last Resort.'

I wanted to take a ferry ride, but I missed the boat.

On the flight to San Francisco I asked the stewardess, "What do you call this desert with my meal?" She replied, "Pie in the sky."

I stepped off of the curb and got that run-down feeling.

When my wife told me that we were going on vacation she sent me packing.

When I called a cab, I had the feeling that I would be taken for a ride.

I wanted to hit the road; instead I beat the pavement.

The bellhop who took my luggage at the hotel said that there would be a carrying charge.

At the airport all of the aircraft were lined up in plane sight.

John took the road less traveled and quickly became lost.

VANITY

Mary was vain; all her efforts were in vain.

VISION

With my dark sunglasses I began to take a dim view of things.

It was visible to the naked eye, invisible if you wore a blindfold.

WAITERS

Waiter: "Is that a party of one, Sir?" Reply: "If it is a party of one it is not much of a party."

I told the waiter, "They also serve who stand and wait."

Busy waiters have a waiting list.

Question to a waiter: Do you wait on the table or do you wait at the table? Answer: Both.

WALL STREET

The stockbroker purchased a pair of long johns and then the bottom fell out.

WEATHER

The weatherman hailed from Alaska.

When the snow began to melt my city started a slush fund.

Phil was left out in the rain, but he was taken in as usual.

Jack was a weatherman, so he knew which way the wind blew.

Was I surprised one night when the tide went out for good?

Is it possible to soak up sunshine?

The rain coming down let up.

Dominic put on the dog, but it was so cold it was a three-dog night.

When it is cold and a small cloud forms as I exhale, I can almost catch my breath.

WEIGHT

Mary lost 15 pounds on the low-calorie diet. Mary reported it lost and now the police are out looking for it.

She was as hungry as a horse, but she ate like a bird.

Luckily Bob was heavy; he liked to throw his weight around.

Mike was so overweight his pants burst at the seams.

On my new diet I lost 130 pounds. Since I weighed 120 pounds at the start I disappeared.

WORK

Pete took a junior college course in finger painting. Pete became upset when he spent three months painting his living room.

Sam was not an actor, but he brought down the house; he was a demolition expert when not acting.

Bill made his bread and butter by selling meat and potatoes at his family's restaurant.

My new supervisor tended to boss me around. I told him that I prefer being supervised rather than bossed. I told my supervisor that my wife specializes in bossing. She is the bosser and I am the bossee.

Firemen don't get tired they just feel burned out.

Joan worked in a bakery. She went to a masquerade party as a tart.

Jack was fired from the chewing gum company; he was caught gumming up the works.

It wasn't exactly a party, but the demolition crew had a blast.

I wanted to sink my teeth into my work, but my teeth were false.

I am used to being out on a limb; I am a tree surgeon.

I used to work for United Parcel Services at Christmas. It was sort of a package deal; part and parcel.

When dealing with dynamite a person with a short fuse is a liability.

I got a part time job on my day off.

I called my rug cleaner on the carpet.

Before the ditch digger quit, he gave it one last ditch effort.

I am out of a job; I'm nobody's fool.

My co-worker advised me to look busy at work; luckily, I had busy work.

Tom did not live by the sweat of his brow; Tom never worked up a sweat.

Do postal workers have a stamping ground? Answer: Yes, it is at the post office.

What's on the agenda for today? What's an agenda?

Jack was not unemployed; he maintained that he was at his leisure.

Bill, the lumberjack, had an ax to grind; it was dull.

I did not know how to get a job cleaning rugs until the rug owner told me to beat it.

Vincent worked in a peanut factory and he was nuts about his job.

The electrician did not get mad; he blew a fuse.

The exterminator did not quit; he merely bugged out.

A tree surgeon did not want to expand his business, but he said that he wanted to branch out.

My barber admitted that his business was a clip joint.

I was working at a lumber company until I got the ax.

I was bagging potatoes until I got the sack.

The seamstress exclaimed, "I'm so excited, I'm on pins and needles."

My roofer said that the roof repair was not free, but it was on the house.

I wasn't out of work, I was just unemployed.

My plumber told me that when he slept, he had pipe dreams.

A skeleton worked his fingers to the bone.

When two seismologists meet each argues by saying, "It's your fault."

I used to be a brown bagger, but today I use plastic bags.

I don't have a brown nose, it's a tan.

The plumber was flush with success.

UPS workers deliver the goods.

Jack wanted to get to the next level, so he decided to take a step down.

What does this red button do? Oh no!

WRESTLING

Bill stopped wrestling; he was tired of someone twisting his arm.

I went to a wrestling match where there were no holds barred.

WRITING

I am on the way to having a runaway bestselling joke book. To date I've sold 20 books.

The handwriting on the wall was graffiti.

What happened was nothing to write home about therefore I decided to telephone.

The critic of my book said that there weren't enough blank spaces or blank pages for that matter.

John's new book was in the works. The problem was that John had gummed up the works.

I wrote a joke book where the table of contents was so long that there was no room left for the jokes to follow.

ZOMBIES

A zombie was dead tired.

When zombies sleep are they dead to the world?

A zombie was totally exhausted and said, "I feel dead on my feet."

The zombie had a deadpan expression.

www.ingramcontent.com/pod-product-compliance
Lightning Source LLC
Chambersburg PA
CBHW020536080526
44583CB00013B/882